101 WAYS
TO
GET MORE
BUSINESS

"It might seem odd to get excited about a business book, but this is the one. It is snappy, inspiring and comes in a workshop style which is quick and easy to read. There are 101 solid ideas for generating more business, many of which are quite inspiring. It is the next best thing to sitting down with a business adviser. I would recommend it to anyone running a service industry, the enthusiasm is quite infectious."

Business Echo

"This book is inspirational – in the best sense. Open it at almost any page and you will find a clear list of 'to dos' and what they will achieve. There's absolutely no waffle, no theory, no academic discussion. Just straightforward techniques for you to apply as they are or amend slightly to fit your particular circumstances. It is a thorough book. It covers everything from analysing your business to prompting bigger sales each time you sell. It's like having your own adviser sitting at your desk to give you the best advice as and when you need it."

Wyvern Business Library

"I would imagine that the title of this book alone should help boost its sales, but it is certainly worth reading. The book is free of padding and the information used is based on real experience."

The Franchise Magazine

"This could well be subtitled 'the art and craft of salesmanship'. The techniques described should assist sales-minded readers considerably to enhance their prospects of business success. All are based on real-life experience."

Business Executive Magazine

"Former Procter & Gamble and Merrill Lynch executive Timothy Foster uses his experience to help facilitate, identify and implement business-building strategies and techniques."

Achievement

101 WAYS
TO
GET MORE
BUSINESS

Timothy R V Foster

**KOGAN
PAGE**

This book is dedicated to my brothers Christopher and Richard

First published in 1992, reprinted 1997

Kogan Page Limited
120 Pentonville Road
London N1 9JN

© Timothy R V Foster 1992

British Library Cataloguing in Publication Data

A CIP record for this book is available from the British Library.

ISBN 0-7494-0760-3

Typeset by DP Photosetting, Aylesbury, Bucks
Printed and bound in Great Britain by
Clays Ltd, St Ives plc

Contents

Prompting Bigger Sales as You Sell   113

Introduction

The period approaching the next millennium has been more challenging for the entrepreneur than any other time in history. We find ourselves moving forward into uncharted territory at the speed of thought. New relationships and national structures have an impact on what we do in ways that may seem strange to us.

New ways of doing business occur every day: new ways of viewing and selecting the merchandise, of placing the order, of paying. New responsibilities and liabilities rest with the seller of goods and services. The course of business is now even more unpredictable than it used to be.

One thing is certain – in order to survive, we must face up to change. Redefinition is the order of the day. Flexibility is the key requirement. An understanding of the consequences of changing events is essential.

This book is for anyone facing the quest for more business. It is intended to enable a quick review of the ways you now go about doing business, and to prompt you in new directions. It is an interactive workbook aimed at facilitating, identifying and implementing effective business-building strategies and techniques. There are:

- 10 ways of building your own credibility
- 12 ways to build a better understanding of your customers
- 13 ways of climbing the ladder of sales success
- 19 ways of improving your prospecting skills
- 7 ways of analysing your existing business
- 12 ways of making things happen by building on relevance
- 9 ways to look at how you come across
- 19 ways to prompt more sales from existing customers

How to Get the Most Out of This Book

The 101 ways outlined here are real, based on real experiences. All the anecdotes actually happened. There's no fluff to pad the book out. It's intentionally lean, to give you fast solutions to your problems.

The mechanisms described here are not intended to be rigid rules. They are meant to be idea prompters. Allow yourself to apply variations as you see fit.

Start by reading the book through, from front to back. That shouldn't take you much more than an hour. Have a pencil or highlighter to hand. When you come across a way that seems useful, circle it. Dog-ear the page. Then go back and see if you can adapt those ideas to your way of doing business. Use them as a launching pad. Some of the ideas may appear familiar to you. Fine. They are there for completeness, so you don't miss anything. I guarantee that some of the concepts will be new to you, and I hope you find these helpful in bringing you the success you so richly deserve.

Building Your Own Credibility

Why do you need credibility? So you will be used. So your services or goods will be in demand. But:

- There's a lot of noise out there – 600 messages a day!
- It's a very competitive world
- There are many hungry competitors
- Competition comes in many forms:
  - Price
  - Service
  - Quality
  - Speed of delivery
  - Uniqueness
  - Experience
  - Knowledge
  - Contacts
  - Resources
  - Brand equity
  - Innovation
  - ?
  - ?

Why should anyone use *you*?
You need to define yourself in your clients' terms. Let's start.

Way 1 Describe what you do

A lot of people have a problem describing what they do in ways that the customer will understand. They may be quite good at doing so in their own terms, but how well does it translate within their prospect's mind?

The problem is that we have a tendency to make assumptions about our customers – that they have a better understanding of our marketplace than they really do, or even that they might actually need us! The exercises on the next few pages work. What they will do is help you shift your definition of yourself or your products and services from an inward-looking point of view to one that respects the mind-set of your customer.

For example, suppose you run a video rental store. Are you in the business of renting videos? Are you a retailer? Are you in the entertainment business? Are you in the leisure business? Do people come to you because they want to rent a video or watch a film?

A friend of mine, whose father owned a restaurant, set up a modest video rental operation in a small parade of shops. But he went one better. He figured he was in the home entertainment business, so he also set up a pizzeria in the back of the shop (see the lateral thinking coming out of the family heritage?). People tend to spend ten or fifteen minutes browsing through the film titles – just long enough to cook a pizza. So most customers come in, drop off their last film, go to the pizza counter, place their order, browse and select a film title, then pick up their pizza. And, of course, the pricing reflects this: 'Large pizza, litre of Coke and a video for £10.' Oh, and he also has a large cinema-style popcorn dispenser for those couch potatoes who want to pretend they're going to the cinema. Needless to say, he's very successful. He's shifted the spend per customer in many cases from maybe £2 a visit to £10 – a fivefold increase.

Start with the worksheet below. It will help you to understand yourself better, and it will help you to present yourself to your prospects and customers more meaningfully.

I am a _____

What does my business card/letterhead/advertising/brochure say about that?

_____

I work in the _____ area/industry/market.

I carry out tasks such as _____

_____

People need my services/goods because _____

_____

_____

If they did not have the kinds of services/goods I offer, they would

_____

_____

_____

The kinds of services/goods I offer are, to my clients/prospects:

☐ Essential   ☐ Useful   ☐ Helpful   ☐ Non-essential
☐ A luxury

Could they carry out/obtain these services/goods for themselves, right now?

☐ Yes   ☐ No

Way 2   SWOT yourself!

A good way of looking at your situation is to do a SWOT analysis. SWOT stands for Strengths, Weaknesses, Opportunities, Threats. SWOT yourself, your product line, your service – whatever works best for you. Use this worksheet. List items at random, put them where they belong, then circle those of greatest importance.

Strengths:

_____

_____

_____

_____

My weaknesses are:

_____

_____

_____

_____

The opportunities open to me are:

_____

_____

_____

_____

The threats to me are:

_____

_____

_____

_____

Now the answers to the questions you need to ask can be driven by these findings:

- **Strengths**

Are you taking full advantage of all your strengths? If you rank them in order of importance, do you give emphasis to the leading strengths? Which of your strengths can be built upon?

Actions I will take on strengths:

Strength	**Action**
_____	_____
_____	_____
_____	_____
_____	_____

• Weaknesses

Are there some weaknesses to which you are avoiding paying attention? If you have been honest with yourself, you may find one or two that could be dealt with more effectively. Ranking them by their impact on your results might point out some suggestions for action.

Actions I will take on weaknesses:

Weakness   **Action**

_____   _____

_____   _____

_____   _____

_____   _____

• Opportunities

Has anything new risen to the surface as a result of this exercise? The advantage of this type of analysis is that hidden factors can come to light as you proceed. What's new?

Actions I will take on opportunities:

Opportunity   **Action**

_____   _____

_____   _____

_____   _____

_____   _____

• Threats

Threats can be external or internal – say the threat of competition, or the threat of losing a key employee, not having enough staff, or having difficulty raising funds for expansion. As the Boy Scouts say – 'Be Prepared'. It's a good idea to redo this analysis every six months or so.

15

Actions I will take on threats:

Threat	Action
_____	_____
_____	_____
_____	_____
_____	_____

Way 3   Identify your competitive advantages

Take a look at what you bring to the party. What makes _you_ competitive? People who compete solely on price may find themselves in a commodity business. This is where the importance of branding comes in. A brand has attributes that surpass mere price considerations, as we will see in Way 4. But first, let's take a look at how you perceive your competitive strengths right now. This worksheet will help you to classify these factors, and there's room to add your own. When you've completed the listing, go back and rank each factor in order of importance to your getting more business.

I can compete on: Relative ranking

Price	☐ Yes	☐ No	_____
Service	☐ Yes	☐ No	_____
Quality	☐ Yes	☐ No	_____
Speed of delivery	☐ Yes	☐ No	_____
Uniqueness	☐ Yes	☐ No	_____
Experience	☐ Yes	☐ No	_____
Knowledge	☐ Yes	☐ No	_____
Contacts	☐ Yes	☐ No	_____

Resources	☐ Yes	☐ No	_____
Innovation	☐ Yes	☐ No	_____
Technical strengths	☐ Yes	☐ No	_____
_____	☐ Yes	☐ No	_____ .

Way 4   Understand what makes brands successful

What is it that makes a brand a hit? An easy way to find out is to evaluate your own favourites. List ten favourite brands/services/organisations. What makes them great for you?

Brand/service/organisation	What makes them great?
_____	_____
_____	_____
_____	_____
_____	_____
_____	_____
_____	_____
_____	_____
_____	_____
_____	_____
_____	_____

Do you notice anything that stands out in the right-hand column? We go through this exercise in my seminars, and the qualities that are dominant, time after time, are customer service, product quality, value for money, and unquestioning acceptance of the fact that the customer is very, very important.

Let me share with you a good example of excellent service. I recently had the exhaust pipe on my car repaired. I looked in the Thomson directory and phoned a company called Mr Exhaust, and they called me back with a quotation based on various possibilities. They were open seven days a week. I decided to use them. When I got there, they invited me to sit in a reasonably comfortable lounge. They told me I'd have to wait 15 minutes before they'd be able to look at my car. There was a coffee machine, a food vendor, a TV and most of the day's newspapers available. The lounge had a window over-looking the workshop area. After about 20 minutes, my car was driven in and put on the hoist. A mechanic inspected it, and then I was invited to come and see for myself. I was politely shown the problem, what worked and what didn't. It was clear what had to be done. I was given the price (it matched the original quote) and told this would take an hour to fix. I said I'd be back.

When I returned an hour later, the car was still on the hoist, but it was being worked on. About ten minutes later, it came off and I was invited to pay my bill. When that transaction was completed, I was given a cardboard portfolio containing a notepad, a Mr Exhaust pen, my bill and guarantee, and a set of stickers for my kids to put on their toy cars (all branded Mr Exhaust, of course!). Even though it had all taken a little longer than suggested, I left there feeling good, and my car sounded much quieter.

How does what you do shape up in these areas?

Way 5   Understand what makes brands fail

Just to prove our point, let's look at the other side of the coin. What is it that makes a brand die? Evaluate your own favourite disasters. List half a dozen dead or dying brands/services/ organisations. What made them fail?

Brand/service/organisation   **What made them fail?**

_____   _____

_____   _____

_____   _____

_____   _____

_____   _____

Here are a couple of my favourites. And I predicted they would fail when they were announced. Why won't people listen?

- Phonepoint. A mobile phone that you could only use for outgoing calls, and only if you were within range of a relay station, identified by a sign on the wall. Such stations were to be found in certain well-populated shopping areas. How much imagination did it take to make this idea up? How many billions were blown? Too many restrictions to its use and no particular incremental benefit (it takes the place of a payphone) despatched this piece of needless technology to an early grave.
- British Satellite Broadcasting, D-Mac, Marco Polo and the Squarial. Coming on the scene some months after the launch of a less complex, more compatible rival system (Sky), BSB was a direct-to-home satellite TV broadcasting facility. It required a dish antenna, a satellite tuner and a converter to make the D-Mac TV signal work on the home TV. The D-Mac TV format was supposed to give a better picture quality, but this was indiscernible on a conventional TV set. BSB spent millions on its own satellite (Marco Polo) and a very fancy headquarters building. Sky leased space on an existing satellite (Astra) and more spartan office space. BSB got into a bidding war with Sky on the prices of movies it had to pay distributors for its movie channel, driving its costs into outer space. BSB's early failure (and merger with Sky to form British Sky Broadcasting) was as predictable as the next sunrise. And now BSkyB is one of the great success stories, with over six million subscribers, expected to rise to nine million by 2000.

Way 6   What is it that makes your *competitors* stand out?

List some competitors. What makes them great for your prospects?

Competitor	What makes them great?
_____	_____
_____	_____
_____	_____
_____	_____

At a recent seminar, I went round the room, asking people to discuss what had come up. One delegate said, 'Well, my competitors use attractive young women as sales reps.' 'Oh, and I suppose you use unattractive young women, is that it?' I couldn't resist replying. It's easy to get a cheap laugh. But, seriously, what are your competitors doing to get the edge on you? Is there something to be learned?

Way 7   What is it that makes *you* stand out?

What makes you great for your clients? What differentiates you?

Feature I offer	Benefit to client . . . and importance
_____	_____
_____	_____
_____	_____
_____	_____

Having taken a look at this, the question arises, are you letting these facts be known? It's all very well to have an edge, but you must also communicate this to your audiences. And keep doing so.

For example, British Airways has done a lot to improve its service over the last few years. Every employee goes through a programme called 'Putting People First', and the results show. I had occasion to complain about some confused boarding instructions that were given to me at Gatwick's new North Terminal a while ago. The passenger agent told me to go to one gate, and the Departure TV listed another gate. The agent was wrong, the TV was right. I almost missed my flight. So I asked for a comment form on the aircraft, and filled out a brief outline of the problem. I handed it to the flight attendant at the other end. A week later, I received a personal letter from Customer Service, apologising for the mix-up and assuring me that the matter was being attended to. Six months later, I received another letter, asking me if I had had the chance to try them again and see for myself if matters had improved. They offered me a voucher good for £50 off my next ticket. It's the constant attention to this kind of detail, the feeling that I am important to them, the sense of care being taken, that makes for good sentiments and a competitive edge.

Way 8 So what *do* you do? Redefine yourself

After you have completed this exercise, try showing it to an independent, unbiased person who does not really know what you do and see if they understand it. Ask them to explain to you what you do, and see if you understand it and if they've got it right. Any gaps between your idea of the reality and their perception must be corrected. Ultimately you want a neutral person to be able to read this and have an absolutely clear idea of what you offer. So keep refining until it is that way.

I am a _____

_____

I work in the _____ area/industry/market.

I carry out tasks such as _____

_____

People need my services because _____

_____

The unique proposition that I bring to the party is:

_____

_____

A client is better off using me/my products because:

_____

_____

In fact, I am:

_____

_____

Way 9   What should be your slogo?

I use the word slogo to define the slogan by the logo. Some people call them straplines. If they're in a TV commercial, they're known as endlines. They form part of the heritage of the brand. Some of them are so famous and well known they immediately conjure up an image of the brand. Try these:

Slogo   **Brand?**

_____ is good for you   _____

The pause that refreshes   _____

The best to you each morning   _____

We try harder   _____

The ultimate driving experience   _____

A good slogo should state a benefit and be relevant to the brand. You should be able to ask for the brand by using the slogo.

Good examples:

- *Taste. Not waist*   Weight Watchers Frozen Foods
- *The antidote for civilisation*   Club Med
- *The best way of expressing*   Zenith Data Systems
  your intelligence
- *As sure as taking it there*   United Parcel Service
  yourself
- *We'll do the homework*   Tricity Bendix

A poor slogo may not work for various reasons – usually because the line sounds like the brand manager talking to his peers. Or because the line is simply meaningless or irrelevant. Who cares? Does this mean I should use it? Try these gems:

Poor examples:

- *All it leaves behind is other non-bios*   Fairy Ultra Detergent
- *Britain's second largest international*   Air Europe
  scheduled airline
- *A company called TRW*   TRW

Write your own slogo:

You   **Slogo**

_____   _____

_____   _____

Is there a benefit in the slogo?

Way 10   Be a specialist

If you are a specialist in whatever you do, you can offer a value-added benefit and price your products and services accordingly. If you are generic, you can only compete on price and delivery. Your credibility will be much better if you have some uniqueness that differentiates you from your competitors.

We are surrounded by niche marketing. A few years ago, the large retailing organisation, The Burton Group, took all the departments that had to do with servicing their shops and offices – like stationery, printing, office furnishings, store fixtures, coat hanger supplies and so on – and rolled them together into a firm called Business Essentials. By consolidating these activities, which had been run variously by all the different retailing subsidiaries, into one cohesive organisation, they were able to put together a very efficient service that would let the stores get back to their real job of retailing, and provide big economies of scale. Then they made Business Essentials into a supplier for other retailers and high street outlets, such as building societies and estate agencies. On their brochure are these words:

> *The successful company of the '90s will target its resources on its core business while contracting-out the distraction of peripheral activity to professional external specialists.*

Companies are getting leaner all the time. They are 'outsourcing' more and more. This means that organisations that can be perceived to replace the now non-existent unit, department or division can find a ready market for their services.

One computer company near London did away with its shipping department and invited Federal Express to come in and run it as one of their branches. Many large organisations contract out their catering. Offices have people who come in and water their plants on a regular basis. Many companies have their car fleets managed by an outside agency. Some big firms have a brand-name travel agency occupying space on the 28th floor to serve all their travel needs.

All these outsourcees are specialists. They do one thing or series of things, they are expert at what they do, and they have an understandable pricing structure.

What does this say to you? Are you a specialist? Do you call yourself a specialist? Could you?

Know About Your Customers and Prospects

A good understanding of your customer will take you a long way to getting more business. This section will help you to develop a better grasp of that most important person. As you go through the exercises, reserve a moment from time to time to look at things from the customer's point of view.

Here's a situation that shows what happens when the customer's point of view is ignored. I was at Gatwick Airport near London, waiting to take the express train to town. I went to the rail ticket counter and asked for a One-day Travelcard. This is a special ticket that lets you travel to London and back, and also entitles you to travel on any of London's buses and underground trains as often as you like at no extra charge, for one day. It is a very good ticket if you are going to do a lot of moving around in the city for a day.

I handed over the money, the man gave me the ticket and presented me with an advertising folder. It was entitled 'LONDON MAP The best of London at a glance'. Perceiving it to be a map, which I did not need or want, I said, 'I don't need this, thank you.' You would expect the man to say, 'OK. Thanks for travelling with us. Enjoy your trip', and take the map back. But no! He said, 'But we're supposed to give one of these to everyone who buys a Travelcard!' So I said, 'What is it, a map?' 'Yeah, it's sort of a map, yeah!' I looked at it. It was a helpful tourist guide: 'Fun ideas and how to get there with a One-day Travelcard.' Fine for tourists. Not of any interest to me. I know my way around London, and I was going there to attend a couple of business meetings. 'No, I don't need it, thank you,' I said, and I handed it back to him. He looked very cross. Why was I spurning his kind offer? He thrust the map back at me (a difficult task because of the bullet-proof glass and high security system cash drawer that protected him from attackers). 'We have to give these to everyone who buys this kind of ticket. Here! Take it and *bin* it!'

He was inviting (no, *ordering*) me to take his company's promotion piece, no matter what. If I didn't want it, I was to throw it away. That's how valuable it was. His perceived role in the equation: deliver one brochure to every buyer of a One-day Travelcard, *or die*! Pay no attention to the needs of the customer. Obey only the edicts of your supervisor.

But what does the customer take away from this? A confirmation of what is already understood – the people who work for the railway are a bunch of unthinking, unfeeling zombies. Privatisation will fix that.

Who is at fault here? Clearly, the railway company's marketing people, for not giving an adequate briefing on the task at hand. It should have gone like this: 'It would be helpful to many of our customers to offer them a map of travel ideas, now that they have a ticket that will get them anywhere.' Good. Makes sense. Good customer service. 'Offer one to each customer who buys one of these tickets.' Note the word *offer*. But they probably said: 'Make sure everyone who buys a ticket gets a map!'

So what is the message? Simply this: Put yourself in the customer's shoes. How would you like to be approached? Do you want to be ordered around or dictated to? How would you like someone to deal with you? When *you* have the answer, then *that* is the answer. Think like a customer! And if that means questioning your concepts, ask the question!

Way 11   Identify who needs you: take a look at your marketplace

Where do your customers come from? How do you find them – do they come to you, or do you have to go to them? Where do you go to identify them?

- Directories
- Internet (World-Wide Web)
- Exhibitions

- Organisations
- Mailing lists
- Personal networking
- Retail outlet
- _____ ?

To know where to look, you need to know who you are looking for. People tend to be grouped together by their characteristics:

- Personal
- Business
- Professional
- Demographics
- Different people need different services – these needs change at different times in their lives

It is change in circumstances that for many people is the most powerful driver of the need for new or different products and services.

The following worksheet will help you to understand these differentiations. Down the left side is a set of personal characteristics. Across the top is space for you to fill in one or more products or services you offer (A, B, C and D). Fill in the appropriateness of the need to the personal characteristic listed, using the following values:

- 1 for a very strong need
- 2 for a moderate need
- 3 for a weak need
- 4 for no need

Then add the figures across on each horizontal line. The lowest numbers indicate the most important personal characteristics. List these characteristics in order of importance to the type of business you want to do on the following page.

Personal characteristics/needs profile

Personal characteristics	Product or service				Totals
	A	B	C	D	
Married					
Single					
School-age children					
Homeowner					
Tenant					
Own business					
Employed					
Self-employed					
Unemployed					
Retired					
Age under 16					
Age 17–21					
Age 22–30					
Age 31–40					
Age 41–50					
Age 51–60					
Age 61–70					
Age 70 +					
Income under £10K					
Income £10–15K					
Income £15–20K					
Income £20–30K					
Income £30–40K					
Income £40–50K					
Income £50–100K					
Social grade A*					
Social grade B*					
Social grade C1*					
Social grade C2*					
Social grade D*					
Social grade E*					
Totals					

* See opposite for social grade definitions

K = 1000
Ratings: 1 = Very strong 2 = Moderate 3 = Weak 4 = Not relevant

Social grade	Social status	Occupation
A	Upper middle class	Higher managerial, administrative or professional
B	Middle class	Intermediate managerial, administrative or professional
C1	Lower middle class	Supervisory or clerical, junior managerial, administrative or professional
C2	Skilled working class	Skilled manual workers
D	Working class	Semi and unskilled manual workers
E	Lowest subsistence level	State pensioners or widows (no other earner), casual or lowest grade workers

Way 12   List who needs you, in order of importance

Take the characteristics that you determined are most appropriate to your offerings from the worksheet in Way 11 and list them in order of importance, according to the ratings you gave them (the smaller the number, the higher their importance). Then show how you can identify these people (directories, organisations, mailing lists, personal networking, retail outlet, etc).

The kinds of people who need my services/goods most are, in order of importance:

Characteristic   **How do you identify them?**

_____   _____

_____   _____

_____   _____

Way 13   Who do you want your customers to be?

In the best of all possible worlds, who would you *like* to be selling to? Remember Basil Fawlty in *Fawlty Towers*, getting so excited because he thought he had a Lord as guest at his hotel? ('I sign my name Melbury because I am *Lord* Melbury.') No more riff-raff for him! Of course, it turned out he was a con man in the end.

Does it matter who your customers should be? Isn't one person's money as good as another's? Of course. But it may be that one type of customer is better for you because they are more knowledgeable, and you don't have to spend so much time explaining things. Or they have more money and might be easier to sell to. Or they have other needs as well that you can also fill. Or they are prestigious. So take a few moments to think about who your ideal customer is:

My ideal customer is (tick everything that applies):

Male ☐ Female ☐   Child ☐   Age: 0–10 ☐   11–16 ☐   17–21 ☐

Age: 22–30 ☐   31–40 ☐   41–50 ☐   51–60 ☐   61–70 ☐   70+ ☐

Education: Incomplete ☐   O Levels/ ☐   A Levels ☐ University ☐
                                 GCSEs

Income group: Under £10K ☐   £10–15K ☐   £15–20K ☐   £20–30K ☐
                £30–40K ☐   £40–50K ☐   £50–100K ☐   £100K + ☐

Married ☐   Single ☐   School-age children ☐

Social grades:*   A ☐   B ☐   C1 ☐   C2 ☐   D ☐   E ☐

K = 1000
*See page 29.

Way 14   Who don't you want?

Obviously you don't want time wasters and tyre kickers. When I was a stockbroker in Toronto, I found one kind of client I didn't want was the kind with a large investment portfolio – 10,000 shares of International Nickel, 1000 IBM, that sort of thing – and all he would do was talk about how he might buy 10,000 more Nickel, or sell the IBM and buy Digital, but he never *did* anything! Since my living was based on transactions, this was dire. I identified this type of client as a stock teaser.

You don't want people who spend hours getting your advice and then go off and buy somewhere else. Or people who buy and then come back some months later and want to return the goods, now worn, because they're not satisfactory. Or people who ask you to submit a proposal on speculation, spend hours in meetings with you and then hire someone else (who they were going to use anyway – they were just fishing for some free thinking).

Surely you know who you don't want to deal with. So make a list of them:

_____

_____

_____

_____

_____

Way 15   Where are they?

Where are your customers? Do they deal with you face to face, or over the phone? Or by mail or fax? Do they come to you or do you go to them? Do you have to do a lot of travelling? Or do they? Let's take a look at the situation.

My customers are located in these areas, and I deal with them by these means ('Visits We/They' means 'we' visit them, and 'they' visit us. 'Presence' means we have a representative, office or agent in that location):

	Visits We/They		Phone	Fax	Mail	Presence	Other
UK	☐	☐	☐	☐	☐	☐	_____
European Community	☐	☐	☐	☐	☐	☐	_____
Europe non-EC	☐	☐	☐	☐	☐	☐	_____
USA	☐	☐	☐	☐	☐	☐	_____
Canada	☐	☐	☐	☐	☐	☐	_____
Mexico	☐	☐	☐	☐	☐	☐	_____
South/Central America	☐	☐	☐	☐	☐	☐	_____
Middle East	☐	☐	☐	☐	☐	☐	_____
Africa	☐	☐	☐	☐	☐	☐	_____
Asia	☐	☐	☐	☐	☐	☐	_____
Far East	☐	☐	☐	☐	☐	☐	_____

Way 16   What are they thinking?

What do you suppose your customers and prospects are thinking *now* about what you offer? Do they know about it, or is it something completely new? Do you have to do a lot of explaining, or do they know what they want right away? Do they know about it as a competitive item but not about you as the purveyor of it? What's the story?

My customers and prospects are currently thinking . . .

● About their needs in this direction:

_____

(They might say, 'I just wish I could . . .

_____

● About what I offer:

_____

- About me as purveyor:

Way 17 What would you like them to be thinking?

Now we get to the best of all possible worlds once again. If you could write the script for the thoughts of your customers and prospects regarding what you offer, what would be running through their minds?

I would like my customers and prospects to be thinking . . .

- About their needs in this direction:

- About what I offer:

- About me as purveyor:

And what else?

Way 18   What do you have to do to get them to think that way?

To get them thinking the way I want, I need to do these things:

- About their needs in this direction:

  _____

  _____

  _____

- About what I offer:

  _____

  _____

  _____

- About me as purveyor:

  _____

  _____

  _____

And what else?

  _____

  _____

  _____

Way 19   What turns them on?

You have to put yourself in your customers' shoes and fantasise about their dreams and aspirations. In the UK we say 'sell the sizzle, not the sausage'. In the USA they say 'sell the sizzle, not the steak'. Either way, it's alliterative! What it means is that people don't buy features, they buy benefits. So you need to have a good understanding of the kinds of benefits your customers go for. What would make them salivate?

If you have an idea of their demographics (see Way 13) or their psychographic profile (personality traits), you can make some reasonably safe predictions. People who come from different identifiable groups tend to behave in certain ways. A middle-aged family man with three children in private schools and a large mortgage will have certain attitudes to high-priced luxury goods that will be quite different from either a retired company director on a good pension, or a young and single successful salesman. Their values and aspirations are different. A widow with five children who is living on family allowance and small part-time earnings is moved by different emotions than a teenage fashion model. A company director of a struggling new business will look at your proposition quite differently from a similarly titled person who works for a large and successful PLC.

So what turns your customers on?

_____

_____

_____

I was sending an important letter to a customer. I wanted to make sure that he received it the next day, but I did not have his postcode. Nor did I have his telephone number. I remembered that the post office had a free postcode service. You telephone them, give them the address, and they tell you the code.

I called the number I had for the post office expecting a typical runaround. Naturally, it was the wrong number. 'Postcodes are on 293552,' said the post office person. 'Here we go,' I thought.

I called the new number, which was answered on the second ring – that was a surprise! 'I need to look up a postcode, please.' 'I'm sorry that line is busy, and there are two people holding.

Do you wish to hold on, or would you prefer to call back?' 'I'll call back,' I said. I gave them ten minutes, and telephoned again. One ring, and they answered. 'I'm sorry that line is busy,' she said. 'How many other people are holding?' I asked. 'You're next,' she said. 'Okay, I'll hold on.' I waited. Thirty seconds went by, and she came back on the line. 'That line is still busy, do you wish to continue to hold?' 'Yes, I'll hold.' Another 30 seconds went by, and, 'I'm afraid that line is still busy. May I have them ring you back?' I couldn't believe my ears! 'Yes, please,' I said. Since when did the post office take this kind of approach to customer service? A few moments later, my phone rang, and we completed the enquiry in a few seconds, prefaced by an apology for keeping me waiting.

Something has happened to the post office, and I like it! They're getting the right attitude towards the customer.

Way 20   What turns them off?

The same ground rules apply as in Way 19. People can feel threatened by new technology, be afraid of computers, risk or uncertainty. How many of these types of threat lie in your proposition?

These are the things that turn my customers and prospects off:

• About their needs in this direction:

_____

_____

_____

• About what I offer:

_____

_____

_____

- About me as provider:

_____

_____

_____

And what else?

_____

_____

_____

Years ago, I lived in Toronto. There was a strange bureaucratic way of selling alcoholic beverages by the bottle. You had to go to a place called a Liquor Control Board of Ontario (LCBO) store where you filled out an order form, specifying the catalogue numbers of the brands you wanted, displayed on listings adjacent to the order desks. Then you took the form, on which you also had to write your name and address, to the cash register to pay. The cashier would ring up a separate order slip for each item, a complex process involving placing many little pieces of paper in the till one at a time and printing out a receipt for each bottle. You took your receipts to the counter, where a team of fully qualified civil servants were waiting to go into the secret section in the back, where the bottles were hidden. They would return with your order, which would be put in a plain brown paper bag, and finally, with some reluctance, handed to you.

One day I was in the store and it was crowded. Of the three cash registers available, one was in use. The other two were silent. At the operating cash register, a line of perhaps 15 people stood. Each order took maybe 30 seconds to process. The outlook was daunting from the end of the queue. Meanwhile, at the counter six shop assistants stood, chatting about last night's hockey game.

After standing in the queue for five minutes, I could take it no longer. 'Why not open up another cash register?' I bellowed. 'It's ridiculous to have everybody standing *here* and everybody standing *there!*' The result was electrifying. First of all, the customers acted embarrassed, that anyone had seen fit to suggest something to ease their lot. Second, the men behind the counter became defensive. 'We're not cashiers!' they said. But suddenly, another cashier was found, and the line broke into two, as some of the suffering clients looked at me with silent thanks.

What are the messages here? First of all, people have long memories about bad service. That event took place 24 years ago, but it feels as if it were yesterday. People talk about bad experiences to their friends at least four times more than they do about good experiences. This means that you need four good experiences to cancel out one bad one. (The LCBO long ago abandoned the the system described above. They now have stores where you can help yourself, and no forms need to be filled out!)

Second, be a part of the solution, not a part of the problem. When you are part of the solution you have a great deal of value. When you are part of the problem, what good are you? Of which part were the people behind the counter at the liquor store? Of which part are you?

When a problem like this comes up, ask yourself the question: 'Am I part of the solution? Or am I part of the problem?' Then act accordingly.

If the men behind the counter had been thinking *customer* instead of *time*, perhaps the service would have been better. Put yourself in your customer's shoes! How do you like to be treated?

Way 21 How do you get to them?

What's the best way for you to reach your customers and prospects? By personal visits? Telephone calls? Letters? Advertising? Signs? Referrals from contacts? Articles in the press? TV programmes? Displays in shops? Word of mouth?

Another worksheet follows. Write in several types of customers and prospects, and identify the best ways of reaching them. Then circle those ways you now use. See anything?

Type of contact   Reached through:

	Personal	Phone	Mail	Ads	Media	Displays	Referrals	Other
Customers								
_____	☐	☐	☐	☐	☐	☐	☐	____
_____	☐	☐	☐	☐	☐	☐	☐	____
_____	☐	☐	☐	☐	☐	☐	☐	____
_____	☐	☐	☐	☐	☐	☐	☐	____
Prospects								
_____	☐	☐	☐	☐	☐	☐	☐	____
_____	☐	☐	☐	☐	☐	☐	☐	____
_____	☐	☐	☐	☐	☐	☐	☐	____
_____	☐	☐	☐	☐	☐	☐	☐	____

Way 22   When's the best time to get to them?

Time here means time of day and time of year. What are the seasonal factors? Remember, if you have a high-tag item you want to sell, you may have to get it built into a budget, and most companies budget for the next year in the fourth quarter of the current year. So a bad time to propose a major expenditure is in the first quarter of a year, and a good time is in the third or fourth quarter.

Then your business may be seasonal – heavy Christmas activity, or heavy summer holiday business. So log your time factors here:

The best times to reach my prospects to produce business are (tick all boxes that apply):

Months of year

Jan	Feb	Mar	Apr	May	Jun	Jul	Aug	Sep	Oct	Nov	Dec	Any
☐	☐	☐	☐	☐	☐	☐	☐	☐	☐	☐	☐	☐

Days of week

Mon	Tue	Wed	Thu	Fri	Sat	Sun	Any
☐	☐	☐	☐	☐	☐	☐	☐

Times of day

Pre 8am	8–9am	9–12am	12–2pm	2–5pm	5–7pm	Post 7pm	Any
☐	☐	☐	☐	☐	☐	☐	☐

Climbing the Ladder of Goodwill

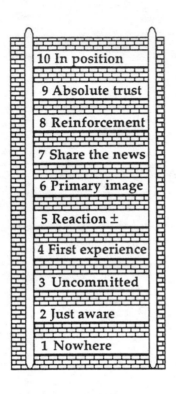

10 In position
9 Absolute trust
8 Reinforcement
7 Share the news
6 Primary image
5 Reaction ±
4 First experience
3 Uncommitted
2 Just aware
1 Nowhere

This is the Ladder of Goodwill. It's an easy way of perceiving how your relationships stand. If you work in something other than the provision of a commodity, where price and delivery are all-important, I'm sure you'll agree that doing business is all about building and maintaining relationships. It's about developing goodwill, equity or involvement for you, your products and your services, among your clients and other contacts.

Whatever you call it, what I mean is that intangible value that you own, that people respect when they think of you, your products or your services. It's the value of your business in patronage, reputation, etc, over and above its tangible assets.

Yes, goodwill is an intangible, and it can become very valuable. Yet it's hard to measure it in financial terms. You can't go out and buy goodwill. You have to get it the old-fashioned way. You have to *earn* it.

Here's how I illustrate the concept of goodwill in my seminars. You have this friend, and you want to buy him or her a birthday present. You are in Debenhams, and you see a display of Sony Walkmans (Walkmen?). The price is right, and the shop assistant will even gift-wrap it for you. So you take it home in its Debenhams carrier bag and think about the gift. You'd like one just like it yourself. You take it out. It's all wrapped up. It would be a shame . . . so you put it back in the bag. But you still want one.

Next day you're in Harrods. There is the Walkman, just the way you want it. Even the price is the same. So you buy one for yourself. 'No, don't bother to wrap it, it's for me.' You take it home in its Harrods carrier bag. Now it's time to take your gift to your friend. You take the gift-wrapped Walkman out of the Debenhams bag and put it in the Harrods bag. And off you go. Harrods have more goodwill than Debenhams.

- Mercedes Benz have more goodwill than Lada
- McDonald's have more goodwill than Wimpy's or Burger Town
- Swissair have more goodwill than Sabena

Where is your goodwill? It's all over the place. You no doubt have excellent personal goodwill with your family or best friends or best customers. You have less personal goodwill with a prospect you're phoning for the first time.

So let's take a trip up the Ladder of Goodwill. This ladder has just ten rungs to take you to the top. On the following pages, we'll see what it means to be on each step of the ladder, and find out the sorts of things people are saying about you at each stage. And we'll discuss how to move up from one step to the next. At the end of this section are some worksheets (Ways 34 and 35) to help you manage this process.

At any moment, you are at a different step on the Ladder of Goodwill with different audiences. On each of the following pages, you can identify people in your audiences who are on the step under discussion.

Although we have ten rungs on the ladder, it is possible to move more than one rung at a time. However, if we do this, the rungs we are jumping over need to be covered in the activities enabling the jump. If you leave a gap in the experience, it can come back to haunt you.

Way 23   Step 1 – Starting out: you are nowhere

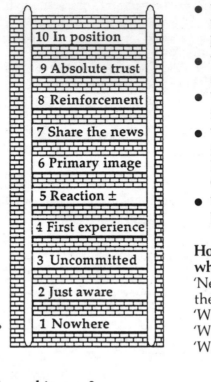

| 10 In position |
| 9 Absolute trust |
| 8 Reinforcement |
| 7 Share the news |
| 6 Primary image |
| 5 Reaction ± |
| 4 First experience |
| 3 Uncommitted |
| 2 Just aware |
| 1 Nowhere |

- You are at the bottom of the ladder.
- Your target does not know of you.
- You are nowhere in their mind.
- You must take the first step up the Ladder of Goodwill.
- You are nothing but 'Who?'

How you know – what they are saying
'Never heard of them.'
'What do they do?'
'Who are they?'
'Where are they?'

Who's on this rung?
Write the names of prospective customers, people, companies or generic groups who fit this category:

_____   _____

_____   _____

_____   _____

_____   _____

_____   _____

_____   _____

What do you have to do to move them up?

- Build awareness for your proposition
- List people or groups who should know about you
  - Users, customers
  - Media – specialist/lay press
  - Influencers, recommenders, advisers, users' associations.
- Build a plan to carry your message, eg
  - Advertising, public relations
  - Brochures, videos, displays
  - Direct mail, cold-call selling, seminars, exhibits
  - Stories/interviews in the media
  - Internet web site

Way 24 Step 2 – You are on the way. Awareness builds

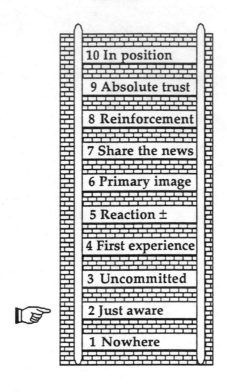

10 In position
9 Absolute trust
8 Reinforcement
7 Share the news
6 Primary image
5 Reaction ±
4 First experience
3 Uncommitted
2 Just aware
1 Nowhere

- The awareness you create is just that.
- It does not mean they understand you.
- It does not mean they trust you.

How you know – what they are saying
'Yes, I've heard of them, but I don't know much about them.'
'Aren't they new?'

Who's on this rung?
Write the names of prospective customers, people, companies or generic groups who fit this category:

_____   _____

_____   _____

_____   _____

_____   _____

_____   _____

_____   _____

What do you have to do to move them up?

- Reinforce awareness and induce trial
  - Provide experience of your offer, demonstrate what it does
- Network among relevant audiences
- Develop ways for people to get to know your proposition, eg
  - Sampling, educational materials
  - Internet web site
- Use relevant activities/locations
- Attend trade shows, exhibits where your audiences gather
- Be seen as the authority who delivers quality

Way 25   Step 3 – The uncommitted

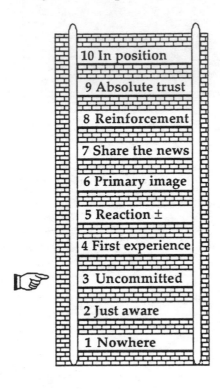

- 10 In position
- 9 Absolute trust
- 8 Reinforcement
- 7 Share the news
- 6 Primary image
- 5 Reaction ±
- 4 First experience
- 3 Uncommitted
- 2 Just aware
- 1 Nowhere

- Your target is aware but not there.
- You are at one of the critical phases.
- Every action either builds upon or destroys your proposition.
- You must be prepared to deliver on their first experience.

**How you know –
what they are saying**
'Yes, I've seen their idea. So what?'
'What's in it for me?'
'OK, you say you're so great. Prove it.'

Who's on this rung?
Write the names of prospective customers, people, companies or generic groups who fit this category:

_____   _____

_____   _____

_____   _____

_____   _____

_____   _____

_____   _____

What do you have to do to move them up?

- Identify your key values and make them known
  - Interactive group participation of key players leads to understanding and ownership of your objectives and values
- Support your proposition in every action
- Tell your audiences, show you care

Way 26 Step 4 – That all-important first experience

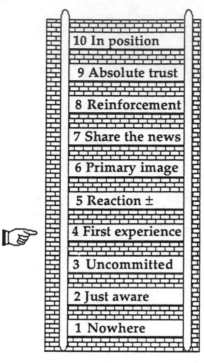

Rung
10 In position
9 Absolute trust
8 Reinforcement
7 Share the news
6 Primary image
5 Reaction ±
4 First experience
3 Uncommitted
2 Just aware
1 Nowhere

- This is the moment of truth.
- You have made great strides.
- You've moved from nowhere to an actual sampling of your proposition.

How you know – what they are saying
'OK, let's give it a whirl.'
'I'll try some and see if it works out.'
'Put me down for one for the moment.'

Who's on this rung?
Write the names of prospective customers, people, companies or generic groups who fit this category:

_____   _____

_____   _____

_____   _____

_____   _____

_____   _____

_____   _____

What do you have to do to move them up?

- Your delivery must be immaculate
- You want to obtain a positive reaction to your proposition
  - Make the experience positive and unforgettable
  - Make sure the proposition is working
  - Exceed expectations
- Provide 24-hour hotline/home telephone number for problems
  - Offer cast-iron guarantees

Way 27 Step 5 – The reaction: positive or negative?

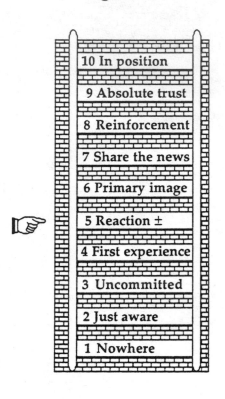

10 In position

9 Absolute trust

8 Reinforcement

7 Share the news

6 Primary image

5 Reaction ±

4 First experience

3 Uncommitted

2 Just aware

1 Nowhere

- Seek reactions to this first experience.
- This will help you to correct any problems and build on your strengths.
- Avoid excuses.
- These reactions will go to building your primary image in your targets' minds.

How you know – what they are saying
'That was excellent. I'm impressed.'
'Well, they didn't deliver on their promise. The whole thing was a disaster.'

Who's on this rung?
Write the names of prospective customers, people, companies or generic groups who fit this category:

_____   _____

_____   _____

_____   _____

_____   _____

_____

What do you have to do to move them up?

- Ask for feedback. 'Were you happy with this?'
  - Provide hotline/fax/home telephone number
  - Provide way to get feedback/comments, eg reply-paid postcard, e-mail
  - User questionnaire/survey (anonymous)
- Reinforce the positive reactions
  - Follow up with visit/phone call/thank you note
  - Gather the responses and put together in a report
  - Publish the report. Use it in ad
- Don't even let a negative reaction occur, but if it does, fix it and fix it fast!
  - Fix first, worry about responsibilities later
  - Go back and make sure they're satisfied

Way 28   Step 6 – Building the primary image

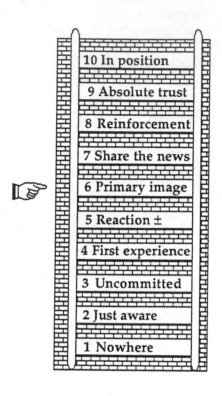

- The accumulation of experiences up to this point establishes a primary image in the mind of your target.
- The image you establish will help to induce further experience of your products and services.
- Or it won't.

How you know – what they are saying
'You know, they're pretty good.'
'They are a perfect example of the kind of thing we need in this area.'
'There should be more like them.'

Who's on this rung?
Write the names of prospective customers, people, companies or generic groups who fit this category:

_____   _____

_____   _____

_____   _____

_____   _____

What do you have to do to move them up?

- Build up a file of positive experiences
  - Make this an important task, assign good people
  - Give it time, resources
  - Keep it up to date
  - Make sure all top internal people are kept informed
- Keep the experience great
  - Make sure all components/people/staff deliver on the promise; stick to your key values
  - Fix problems fast
  - Feed back to your people. Celebrate!

Way 29 Step 7 – Sharing the news

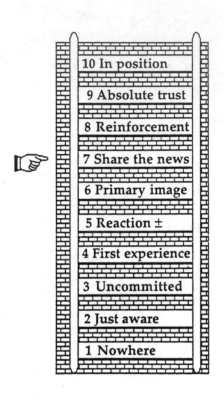

- Research shows that people tend to share bad experiences four times as much as good experiences.
- This means one bad experience can cancel out four good ones.
- Don't rely on your targets to share the news. You must do it.

How you know – what they are saying
'Let me tell you about my experience with . . .'
'If you want a good result, try . . .'
'These people are hopeless. Don't waste your time.'

Who's on this rung?
Write the names of prospective customers, people, companies or generic groups who fit this category:

_____   _____

_____   _____

_____   _____

_____   _____

What do you have to do to move them up?

- Take the positive experiences and let others know
  - Let people (customers/staff/suppliers) know what's going on, eg newsletters/briefing sessions/personal contact/ telephone calls, interviews, stories in relevant media, Internet web-site
- Get the people who buy your proposition to act as your ambassadors
  - Make your best customers your allies

Way 30   Step 8 – Reinforcement of things past

10 In position

9 Absolute trust

8 Reinforcement

7 Share the news

6 Primary image

5 Reaction ±

4 First experience

3 Uncommitted

2 Just aware

1 Nowhere

- This is where you build on the foundations you have now laid.
- The more positive the past experiences, the more powerful will be the bond you build.
- You are getting close to a relationship based on absolute trust.

How you know – what they are saying
'You seem to have anticipated my needs.'
'You really understand my problems.'

Who's on this rung?
Write the names of prospective customers, people, companies or generic groups who fit this category:

_____   _____

_____   _____

_____   _____

_____   _____

_____   _____

What do you have to do to move them up?

- Turn a good feeling about your product/service into an excellent one
  - Don't stop
  - Make sure the second, third . . . nth involvement with *existing* customers maintains the standards of one with a new customer
  - Show them you still care, even though they're already sold
  - Take them to lunch, a show, give them a thank-you event

Way 31 Step 9 – Absolute trust, or on being almost perfect

- When you have the condition of absolute trust, you can have a disaster, and it seemingly won't matter.
- But it does matter, so avoid disasters.
- You are nearly at the top of the ladder, but you can still fall off, and it's a long way down!

How you know – what they are saying
'These people will absolutely deliver for you. You have no worries.'
'I do not hesitate in recommending them.'

Who's on this rung?
Write the names of prospective customers, people, companies or generic groups who fit this category:

_____   _____

_____   _____

_____   _____

_____   _____

What do you have to do to move them up?

- Maintain the relationship at all times
  - Always anticipate needs and deliver evidence of this vigilance on your part
- Never let more than *one* month go by without a personal 'touch' with your key contacts (visit/letter/phone call/e-mail)
  - Think of ways to *keep* in touch
- Scour the media for reasons to show you are thinking about them
  - Find a reason (eg competitive news) and phone
  - Be the second most informed person about the contact's business (she/he is the first)

Way 32   Step 10 – Sitting on top of the world

```
☞   10 In position

     9 Absolute trust

     8 Reinforcement

     7 Share the news

     6 Primary image

     5 Reaction ±

     4 First experience

     3 Uncommitted

     2 Just aware

     1 Nowhere
```

Congratulations.
You are where the
leaders are:

- Mercedes Benz
- Harrods
- McDonald's
- Federal Express
- Concorde
- You

**How you know –
what they are saying**
'Why fool around
with anyone else?'
'Let me tell you why
they are so good.'
'They are the best.
Full stop.'

Who's on this rung?

Write the names of prospective customers, people, companies
or generic groups who fit this category:

_____   _____

_____   _____

_____   _____

_____   _____

_____   _____

_____   _____

What do you have to do to keep them there?

- Follow all the steps that got you where you are today
  - Maintain the positive relationship
  - Keep proving your fans to be right
- Bring the laggards in your targets to the top
  - Different people are at different steps on your Ladder of Goodwill at any one time
- Periodically analyse all contact relationships and . . .
  - Keep moving the lower ones up, while keeping the top ones on top

Way 33   Goodwill Ladder worksheet

Based on your analysis of those ten steps of the Ladder of Goodwill, use this worksheet to record how you want to progress your contacts. Ideally, you should use a computer spreadsheet to manage this process.

Contact	Current rung	Target rung
_____	_____	_____
_____	_____	_____
_____	_____	_____
_____	_____	_____
_____	_____	_____
_____	_____	_____
_____	_____	_____
_____	_____	_____
_____	_____	_____

Ways 34 and 35 are worksheets to help you manage the process of communication with your contacts. They show the sort of information you should be gathering to ensure that your communications reflect the right level of knowledge about your contacts. Use these as a format for developing or modifying your own records.

Way 34   Networking worksheet

Name _____ Sec'y/PA _____

Company _____

Address _____

_____

_____ Postcode _____

Telephone _____ Fax _____

Direct line _____ Home _____

Car _____ Mobile _____

E-mail _____ Web-site _____

Referred by _____

Birthday _____ Spouse _____

Children _____

Interests _____

Hobbies _____

Networks _____

Car notes _____

Education _____

Home _____

Notes _____

Ladder of Goodwill rung: 1 2 3 4 5 6 7 8 9 10

Referrals:

Name	Telephone	Link
_____	_____	_____
_____	_____	_____
_____	_____	_____
_____	_____	_____

Way 35   Networking logsheet

Name _____   Sec'y/PA _____
Company _____

Date	Event	Remarks	Next action
_____	_____	_____	_____
_____	_____	_____	_____
_____	_____	_____	_____
_____	_____	_____	_____
_____	_____	_____	_____
_____	_____	_____	_____
_____	_____	_____	_____
_____	_____	_____	_____
_____	_____	_____	_____
_____	_____	_____	_____
_____	_____	_____	_____
_____	_____	_____	_____
_____	_____	_____	_____
_____	_____	_____	_____
_____	_____	_____	_____
_____	_____	_____	_____
_____	_____	_____	_____
_____	_____	_____	_____
_____	_____	_____	_____
_____	_____	_____	_____
_____	_____	_____	_____
_____	_____	_____	_____
_____	_____	_____	_____

Prospecting for Business

What do you need to do to get more business?
PROSPECT for it!

Foster's 10 rules of prospecting

1 You've got to prospect to survive
2 You've got to make the contacts
3 You've got to rise above the noise
4 You've got to get in to see people
5 You've got to show them what you offer
6 You've got to show you're a good potential partner
7 You've got to follow up
8 You've got to keep in touch
9 You've got to stay top of your prospect's mind
10 You've got to do it all the time

On the following pages, you will find a series of ways to develop this idea, starting with these rules, outlined with objectives and strategy. And with each rule, we introduce the concept of the *factoid*. My dictionary doesn't define that word yet. But it defines 'oid' as a suffix meaning 'like' or 'resembling'. So I guess we can define a factoid as something like a fact. My factoids are a collection of thoughts that I've gathered over the years, and they are offered here to give extra insight into the prospecting rules. Here's my favourite factoid:

- Success isn't a destination, it's a journey

Way 36 Rule 1 – You've got to prospect to survive

No matter how secure you feel, you will continually lose customers. How?

- Your principal contact leaves and goes somewhere else, or is fired, or dies, to be replaced by a person who doesn't know you and for whom you are NIH (not invented here)
  - This means you have to sell yourself in all over again
  - Of course, the client may become a useful contact at his or her new place of work

Objective

- To ensure a steady flow of new business

Strategy

- Structure a method of developing business and stick to it, even in good times – this book should help
- Make developing new business one of your main goals

Factoids

- Goals start behaviours; consequences maintain them
- A goal is a dream with a deadline

Way 37   Rule 2 – You've got to make the contacts

You have to see the right people – a lot of organisations or potential customers. Not everyone will buy, so you must see many in order to increase your odds of doing business.

Objective

- To identify the right people to contact – aim as high as possible
  - Decision makers
  - Buyers
  - Users
  - Influencers

Strategy

- Use trade directories
  - Go to the library, check the Internet
- Read the trade press; look for opportunities
- Develop your own mailing list of key people, their personal assistants (PAs), phone numbers, e-mail, etc.
- Get listed yourself – people do phone
- Get an Internet web-site
- Make at least ten prospecting phone calls a day
- Be nice to people, especially secretaries and PAs

Factoid

- 'You don't have to be nice to people on the way up if you know you're not coming back down again.'
  Daddy Warbucks in *Annie*

Way 38 Rule 3 – You've got to rise above the noise

Objective

- To communicate in a memorable and effective way – have something unique to offer: your unique selling proposition (USP)

Strategy

- Use relevant and original communications
- Be there when your customers need you; anticipate needs

Factoid

- According to Starch, the research company, consumers are exposed to 623 advertising impressions every day, of which they only remember nine favourably one day later
- That means 69 out of 70 messages are wasted

Way 39   Rule 4 – You've got to get in to see people

Objective

- To make an appointment with the right person (aim high)
  - To show your work
  - To identify opportunities
  - To leave a positive impression

Strategy

- Use simple actionable device, eg
  - Postcard with stamp on it
  - Fax response mechanism
  - Fax form on back of letter
  - Small appropriate gift that demands a note of thanks
- Follow up with phone calls, set a date
  - Confirm by mail, fax, e-mail

Factoid

- Avoid reconfirming an appointment on the same day – it's too easy for people to cancel!

Way 40   Rule 5 – You've got to show them what you offer

Objectives

- To show work that could prompt a deal
- To show your USP

Strategy

- Use real examples and present them in person
- Show them in the most relevant order; don't show everything

- Highlight aspects relevant to the audience in the room
- Use examples to prompt questions that drive needs
- Be loaded with case histories to demonstrate knowledge and experience
- Control the meeting

Factoid

- You're only as good as your last screw up

Way 41   Rule 6 – You've got to show you're a good potential partner

Objectives

- To eliminate the fear of the unknown
- To show your cooperative nature, but that you're not a yes person

Strategy

- Seek earliest possible involvement, at the pitch level, if possible
- Offer to work on speculative approaches for them, ideally for a fee
  - Leading to the job
- Describe how you like to work
- Ask questions, show interest, take notes
- Be accessible – home phone, answerphone, mobile phone, pager, fax, e-mail

Factoid

- Asking smart questions shows you're smart more than saying you're smart

Way 42   Rule 7 – You've got to follow up

Objectives

- To thank your contacts for their time, leave a good taste
- To confirm points discussed
- To reinforce key selling points that surfaced
- To fatten your file

Strategy

- Send letter or e-mail next day
- Send something else in two months or so

Factoid

- Help people to get the good feelings they want about what they saw and heard

Way 43   Rule 8 – You've got to keep in touch

Objective

- To keep in touch without being a nuisance
  - To talk to the decision maker, not the PA
  - To probe for opportunities
  - To develop something that requires follow-up

Strategy

- Develop a reason to phone, and a reason to phone back
- Send notes, clippings, faxes
- Make them want to talk to you
- Socialise

Factoids

- It's not the third call that wins the business. It's more like the *twenty-third*!

- 67 per cent of business deals are concluded out of the office

Way 44   Rule 9 – You've got to stay top of your prospect's mind

Objectives

- To be the first person your prospects think of
- To be accessible
- To be *knowledgeable*

Strategy

- Develop ways to keep in front of them
  - Speeches
  - Turn the speeches into magazine articles
  - Conduct research; involve them in it
- Build a network of journalists who write about your subject
  - Phone them with ideas; *they need them*
- Have your own Internet Web-site
- Cross-pollinate
  - Network in related areas
  - Phone with ideas that are not related to your selling something
- Be the second-best informed person on their business

Factoid

- If you say something with enough authority, in a few months it's going to be quoted back to you

Way 45   Rule 10 – You've got to do it all the time

Objective

- Never to let a day go by without some prospecting activity

Strategy

- Make even a quick phone call while you're waiting to meet someone else
- Remember it's a numbers game
  - Keep making the calls and you'll develop the business
  - And never forget to ask for at least three referrals

Factoid

- I know it works in practice, so let's see if it works in theory

Way 46   Prioritise your prospects

If you are working several prospects (or several dozen) at once, it's helpful to prioritise them in order of urgency. You might have an 'A List' and a 'B List'. Or an 'A, B and C List'. You might have 'Long-term prospects' and maybe 'Suspects'. And of course your 'Network'.

'As' are the people who you are working on right now, and who are most likely to give you business in the next few days or weeks. People who you have pitched to and who have to get back to you. People who you'll pitch to this week. They'll either become customers very soon or they'll slip into another prospect category.

'Bs' are those who you are working on, and for whom you haven't yet structured a proposition. Maybe they'll become 'As', or maybe they'll become 'Cs'.

Long-term prospects and 'Cs' are similar. The difference to me is that long-term prospects may only receive your attention at irregular intervals – they may be people to whom you've pitched and lost, or others who have become inactive. 'Cs' you haven't lost yet; they're just lower priority.

Suspects are ideas. Maybe you've heard of someone who does something in which you could be involved. You need to research the background. They are merely suspicions of a prospect. Your objective is to convert them to one of the other categories.

Network is that category of people who don't give you business directly but who know people who can give you business – you might think of them as influencers or referrers. They may be competitors, or former business colleagues. They may be former clients who have moved on, or former employees. Whoever they are, they are critically important, and should be treated with the same sense of importance as your business prospects.

This is how your frequency of contact or consideration of contact should work out:

Category	Frequency of contact or review for contact	Objective
A List	Daily to weekly	Make a customer
B List	Weekly to monthly	Move to A List
C List	Monthly	Move to A or B List
Long-term prospects	At least quarterly	Move to A, B or C List
Suspects	As it happens	Move to A, B or C List
Network	At least monthly	Intelligence

Way 47 Get to know your prospects

The more you know about your prospects, the better will be your opportunities to do business. I'm talking about personal information, such as their hobbies, interests, family facts and so on. Use the forms in Ways 34 and 35 to help you keep track of this sort of data.

Way 48 The prospect of your dreams

Imagine that in tomorrow's post you receive a letter offering you your absolutely best, most magnificent, ideal, superb, appropriate project, assignment or piece of business. You couldn't ask for anything better!

Who is the letter from?

Name: _____

Organisation: _____

What is the deal?

_____

_____

_____

What do you have to do to make it happen?

_____

_____

_____

_____

What are the barriers?

_____

_____

_____

So what are you going to do?

_____

_____

This exercise can produce some amazing results for you. If you give yourself permission to get the ideal kind of project or piece of business, you can find new opportunities opening up that you may have pooh-poohed as being unachievable. Yet anything is achievable. All you have to do is identify the goal, establish what you have to do to get there, and do it.

This is one of the most popular exercises at my seminars, and some of the realisations that surface are a delight to behold.

An awful lot of what gets done gets done because somebody said 'Let's do it'. President Kennedy set the goal of putting a man on the moon by the end of the 1960s. It was done. Rupert Murdoch decided to build a new TV network, came up with the ways to get around restrictive and protective legislation, and did it with Sky TV. Fred Smith avowed that the best way to move millions of packages around the USA was by a hub and spoke system using his own aircraft, where everything was flown to Memphis, sorted and then flown to its destination. The result was Federal Express, and it is now the model for all the other courier services.

So identify the result you want to achieve, ask the magic question 'What do we have to do to get there?' and do it.

Way 49   Revisit your business card file

Who do you know? Have you gone to the trouble of analysing your contacts lately? Do you go out of your way to meet new people? Haven't met anyone new lately? Well, what do you do with all those business cards people keep giving you? Would it be worth your while going through them again? I'll bet if you have 100 cards, you'd find ten people to call whom you'd forgotten about. What about your old personal telephone directories and diaries? Go through them. One of those calls could be very productive.

Way 50   Make one extra contact a day

You will increase your new business by increasing your customer-contact rate. Every contact with a potential customer is an opportunity to obtain an order. Every non-contact is a lost opportunity that can never be recovered. So look at the number of contacts you're making each day, and make one more than you have been. Since it is a numbers game, you will surely do more business.

Way 51   Relevant direct mail can be memorable

A recent issue of *Marketing* magazine quoted some interesting research. According to the US research company Starch, consumers only remember favourably 1.4 per cent of advertising messages one day later (see Way 38). Yet a mailing to a file of frequent flyers was recalled by 74 per cent after three months. This type of impact was confirmed by a mailing on cosmetics to another relevant audience, where 70 per cent recalled it after three months.

The list is all-important. And so is the relevance of the message to the audience. Think of your dearest hobby or pastime. Now imagine a really interesting piece of news that was mailed to you cold – would you feel responsive? Probably. It's that type of impact you should be striving for in any mailing you do.

I did a mailing to outplacement agencies – consultants who work for companies and deal with people who have been made redundant by helping them to relaunch themselves. I wanted to promote my book *101 Ways to Succeed as an Independent Consultant* as a useful piece of literature for such people. On the back of the letter, I put a specially designed fax form, inviting the addressee to reply by simply ticking the boxes on the form and faxing it back to me. I got a 35 per cent response rate. Typical direct mail gets a 1 to 2 per cent response rate.

The easier it is for addressees to reply, the better reply rate you will have.

Way 52 Read the trade magazines and look for provocative information

Every industry has its literature – the trade press. If you've been in business a while, you unquestionably receive some publications free (it's called controlled circulation, which means the publisher controls who gets it). On the principle of you get what you pay for, quite a few people I know never even open these publications, or give them only the most cursory of glances. I'm suggesting that, since some people have gone to the trouble to put together a publication for you, the least you can do is return the favour and look at it. You may be amazed at the ideas you get.

Better still, read the trade journals of other industries. Like those of your customers. If you sell computers, and you're trying to reach accountants, read the accountants' magazines. A good business library will have scores of these available for perusal. When you make a sales call on someone who's in an industry away from your own, ask for some back numbers of his or her industry's literature that you see lying around the office: 'I'd like to know more about the business. Have you any back numbers of this magazine I could have? What do you think is the best magazine for your subject?'

Way 53   Write for the trade magazines of your business

Make a point of getting to know the editors of the trade journals in your industry. Then suggest articles for their publication that you could write. If you can't write, hire a freelance writer to ghost it for you. What you want is your name on the byline of a story relevant to your business, so that you will become associated with the subject as an expert. You'll be quoted. And you can use reprints of the article in your own promotion.

I developed an idea of building a database of advertising slogans – slogos (see Way 9). So I started collecting them and, when I had several hundred, proposed to *Marketing* magazine a weekly competition called 'Name That Brand'. In this, we'd list 10 slogos and 12 possible brands and invite people to match them up. This ran for over a year, and led to the formation of a business that checks slogos for advertisers – The Slogo Register <http://www.thebiz.co.uk/slogos>. Having my name in each issue helped me to build my own credibility and led to more business.

Way 54   Prospecting development worksheet

Use this to help you manage your prospecting initiatives.

What am I going to concentrate on today? Date _____

_____

_____

_____

Which clients/prospects will I target?

_____

_____

_____

What action shall I take?

_____

_____

_____

What barriers will I encounter?

_____

_____

_____

What kind of help will I need?

_____

_____

_____

_____

Analyse Your Business

Every so often take a look at the business you're doing and see where it's coming from. You can do this by sales volume (in monetary terms or in units) and, if you have sophisticated enough records, by profitability. If you use a computer spreadsheet, you'll find it easy to manipulate the figures.

Way 55　Understand the 80/20 rule

Most people find that 80 per cent of their business comes from 20 per cent of their customers.

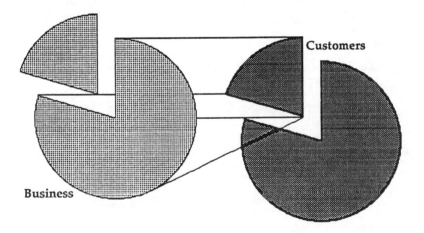

Naturally, it follows that 80 per cent of their customers give them 20 per cent of their business. And yet, all too often, they find they spend most of their time dealing with the vast array of customers who give them the least amount of business. This is called overservicing. Of course, small customers can be grown into large ones, and you should concentrate on the high-potential ones. But spending a lot of time and energy on

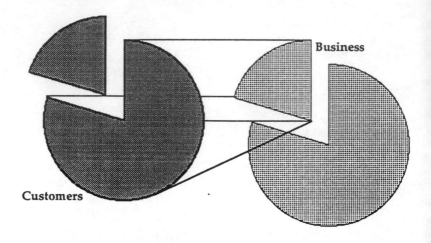

people who give very low rates of return is inefficient, and may be causing unknown amounts of unhappiness with the big hitters.

Way 56   Rank your customers by sales

Let's look at an example of sales analysis. You bring up your last six months' activity and you see this, listing the clients alphabetically:

Client	Sales	Percentage
ABC Co	475	1
DEF Co	1900	5
GHI Co	400	1
HIJ Co	400	1
JKL Co	12755	37
MNO Co	2600	8
PQR Co	802	3
STU Co	400	1
VWX Co	115	0
YZA Co	14808	43
Total	**34655**	**100**

The information starts to be more meaningful when you sort it in descending order by sales (note the 80/20 rule shows up):

Client	Sales	Percentage
YZA Co	14808	43
JKL Co	12755	37
MNO Co	2600	8
DEF Co	1900	5
PQR Co	802	3
ABC Co	475	1
GHI Co	400	1
HIJ Co	400	1
STU Co	400	1
VWX Co	115	0
Total	**34655**	**100**

And you can tell the computer to make a chart:

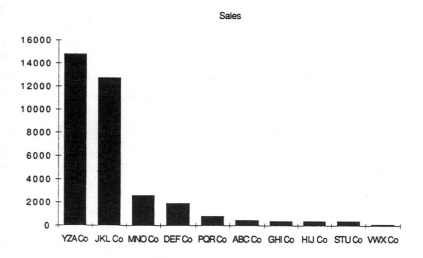

What do you get from this? Well, you can see who your most important customers are. Look at the amount of time you're spending on each, and make any adjustments you think are necessary – devoting more time to the ones giving you the most business.

Way 57   Look at the trends

Taking a look at the trends is very helpful. Call up your sales for the last six months, and compare them with sales for the previous six months. To keep it simple we've kept the same client list. Alphabetically it could look like this. The index figure represents an increase or decrease in activity over the period, with figures lower than 100 being a decrease and higher being an increase:

Client	Previous 6 months	Last 6 months	Change	Index
ABC Co	475	475	0	100
DEF Co	5600	1900	–3700	34
GHI Co	300	400	100	133
HIJ Co	400	400	0	100
JKL Co	12000	12755	755	106
MNO Co	1800	2600	800	144
PQR Co	750	802	52	107
STU Co	500	400	–100	80
VWX Co	100	115	15	115
YZA Co	8400	14808	6408	176
Total	**30325**	**34655**	**4330**	**114**

Once again, this becomes more meaningful if you sort the information, let's say by index in descending order. This gives you the clients with the best increase at the top, and the worst performers at the bottom:

Client	Previous 6 months	Last 6 months	Change	Index
YZA Co	8400	14808	6408	176
MNO Co	1800	2600	800	144
GHI Co	300	400	100	133
VWX Co	100	115	15	115
PQR Co	750	802	52	107
JKL Co	12000	12755	755	106
ABC Co	475	475	0	100
HIJ Co	400	400	0	100
STU Co	500	400	–100	80
DEF Co	5600	1900	–3700	34
Total	**30325**	**34655**	**4330**	**114**

The result prompts a lot of questions that can point to ideas to develop more business. Questions like these:

- What did you do to get YZA to increase sales so well?
- What did you do with MNO?
- And what on earth happened with DEF?
- What do we have to do to turn JKL into a growth situation? And so on.

Way 58   Look at your selling time vs revenues

If you sell a variety of items, analyse your sales time for each type or category while considering the revenues produced. Then allocate your time in the most rewarding area. Let's look at an example. We have four basic items (stereos? computers? insurance policies? whatever). Some are a little more complicated than others, so they take a little longer to sell. The headings on your spreadsheet might look like this:

Item	Units sold	Unit revenue	Revenues	Selling time (hours)	Time/ Unit	Revenue/ Hour
As	100	100	10,000	50	0.5	200
Bs	500	200	100,000	500	1.0	200
Cs	500	400	200,000	250	0.5	800
Ds	100	500	50,000	50	0.5	1000
Total	1,200	300	360,000	850	0.7	420

By dividing the selling time by the units, we get the selling time per unit. As, Cs and Ds all take half an hour each to sell. Bs take an hour each to sell. The average sale takes 0.7 of an hour or 42 minutes.

By dividing the revenues by the selling time in hours we arrive at the revenue per hour. As and Bs both bring in £200 per hour of selling time, while Cs bring in £800 and Ds a whopping £1000 an hour.

Conclusions:

- How can we sell more Ds?
- What can we do to reduce the selling time spent on Bs and As?
- What do you come up with?

Take a look at your own business in the light of this example.

Way 59   How's business?

Examine how your business is made up. The more ticks you have in column A, the better it will be. So if you find many ticks in column C, what do you have to do to shift them to the left? You'll find plenty of room to add your own evaluation points. When you do, keep with the concept – the best situation in column A, the worst in column C.

	A	B	C
The need for my services/goods is	☐ Broad	☐ Moderate	☐ Narrow
The need for my services/goods is	☐ Growing	☐ Static	☐ Declining
– in a recession	☐ Growing	☐ Static	☐ Declining
– in a turnaround	☐ Growing	☐ Static	☐ Declining
– in a boom	☐ Growing	☐ Static	☐ Declining
My competition is	☐ Limited	☐ Moderate	☐ Extensive
Typical selling cycle is	☐ Short	☐ Moderate	☐ Long
Simultaneous customers/projects?	☐ Many	☐ Some	☐ Few/none
Profitability to me is	☐ High	☐ Moderate	☐ Low
_____	☐ _____	☐ _____	☐ _____
_____	☐ _____	☐ _____	☐ _____
_____	☐ _____	☐ _____	☐ _____
_____	☐ _____	☐ _____	☐ _____
_____	☐ _____	☐ _____	☐ _____
_____	☐ _____	☐ _____	☐ _____

Way 60   Clarify your selling cycle

Have you looked at your own selling cycle? What are the
events that have to take place before the customer gets the
goods or service and you get the money? Some transactions
are immediate, such as buying an evening newspaper from a
street vendor on your way home each night. Others are
purchases requiring a lot of consideration – buying a new car
or a house, for example. The newspaper takes a few seconds
and is mostly a reflex action. The second might take weeks or
months.

The longer the selling cycle, the more the opportunity to
lose the deal. In a house purchase, you could see the following
types of event taking place, with plenty of intrusions possible
that could affect the transaction:

- Decision or need to move and obtain new house
- Identification of area(s) to target for new house
- Establishment of price range
- Definition of requirements
- Selection of estate agent(s)
- Review of possible candidates
- Selection of short list
- Comparison of options
  - Schools/Shopping/Commuting
  - Property attributes
- Final selection
- Price offer/negotiations
- Agreement reached
- Property inspection
- Need to obtain a mortgage – interest rate activity
- Need to obtain life insurance – medical examination
- Need for secondary financing
- Ability of buyer or seller to complete dependent transaction
  (another house must be sold or bought to enable this one to
  move – creating a chain)

- Legal or title considerations
- Need for refurbishment/repairs, etc.
- Contract exchange

Look at how many times there could be an event that affects the outcome. Look at all the different opportunities to cause a change of mind.

Now consider your own business activity. What's your business cycle like? What are the opportunities to touch the customer before, during and after the purchase? If you haven't done this before, here's a technique:

- Use 3" × 5" index cards, or a computer program that lets you organise ideas (a word processor will do)
- Put down each step in your business cycle on a separate card or line of the program
- When you feel you have most of the steps, start shuffling them around until they are in a logical sequence
- Identify the ways and occasions when there could be an influence on the outcome
  - Append these to the steps
  - Look at whether you are controlling those steps you can control
- Take the appropriate action

Here's an example. I want to write a new book. Here are the steps involved, as they came to mind, in any order:

- Decide to write new book
- Determine competition – has it been done?
- Identify working title
- Identify prospective publisher(s)
- Write outline of book contents
- Define the audiences
- Talk to friends and network about possible appeal

- Identify potential bulk purchasers
- Research book contents
- Propose to publisher
- Write first draft of book
- Negotiate contract
- Visualise the book, size, look, illustrations
- Obtain visuals if necessary
- Do index
- Revise text according to editorial comments
- Publish and promote!

Now shuffle the items around until they make a logical sequence:

- Decide to write new book
- Identify working title
- Determine competition – has it been done?
- Write outline of book contents
- Define the audiences
- Visualise the book, size, look, illustrations
- Talk to friends and network about possible appeal
- Identify potential bulk purchasers
- Identify prospective publisher(s)
- Propose to publisher
- Negotiate contract
- Research book contents
- Write first draft of book and submit it
- Obtain visuals if necessary
- Revise text according to editorial comments
- Do index
- Publish and promote!

Then put a time-scale to it, for example:

Week 1	• Decide to write new book
	• Identify working title
	• Determine competition
Week 2	• Write outline of book contents
	• Define the audiences
	• Visualise the book
	• Talk to friends and network
	• Identify potential bulk purchasers
	• Identify prospective publisher(s)
Week 3	• Propose to publisher
Week 7	• Negotiate contract
	• Research book contents
Week 12+	• Write first draft of book and submit it
	• Obtain visuals if necessary
Week 16	• Revise text
Week 18	• Do index
Week 30	• Publish and promote!

The above time-scale is fairly typical for a simple book such as the one you are reading. Now let's look at the ways you can touch the customer. Who is the customer? In this case, several entities meet that description:

- Publisher prospects
- The publisher who agrees to do it
- Book shops (secondary contact – it's really the publisher's job)
- Possible bulk purchasers
- Possible reviewers and influencers
- Individual buyers

Timing is everything. When I lived in the USA, I wrote a book called *The Aircraft Owner's Handbook*. Because of my contacts, I was able to negotiate the sale of 13,000 copies of the book to the Aircraft Owners and Pilots Association as a membership premium ('Join AOPA and get this great book free!'). This was done after publication. Later I wrote a sequel – *The Aviator's Catalogue* – and went back to AOPA in advance of publication. I sold 12,000 copies before it came off the press, making a cool $24,000 on the deal. Because I was able to offer the book before printing, I was able to obtain an excellent price for them which clinched the deal.

Ready to clarify your selling cycle? Over to you:

- What are the steps?
- In what sequence should they be listed?
- What are the timing considerations?
- With whom are the selling interfaces?
- Who can make an impact on those interfaces?

Way 61   You may be in the property business and not even know it

If you have a restaurant (if you don't, you can still use this thinking, so stay with us!), you have a certain amount of space devoted to tables and chairs where your customers sit. And you have other areas devoted to food preparation, dishwashing, money handling, bar services, washrooms and so on. The productive areas are the tables and chairs. Everything else is support.

When your customers come in for a meal, they occupy some of this space for a period of time, while they feed and imbibe. Then they leave, depositing some money or its plastic equivalent in your till. Have you ever thought about this as a short-term property rental? They have rented the table and chairs for perhaps one or two hours. If you are a high-class establishment, dealing with top-quality food and wines, you may have been able to extract £30 to £50 or more from each tenant. A fully occupied four-seater table may have brought you in £200 rent in two hours. If you multiply out all your space with the typical yields per area, you'll get an idea of the hourly rate you are earning per seat.

How can you increase the yield from a fixed amount of space without increasing prices? By increasing the turnover. How can you increase the turnover? By putting the tables to work for longer hours or by having more people rent them from you in a given period of time. Some restaurants have two sittings – say at dinner, a 7 pm sitting and a 9 pm sitting – instead of 'When can you get here?' In Europe, people don't seem to go to lunch until 1 pm or even later. In North America, many people go to lunch at noon. So it is easier to have two sittings there, thus increasing the yield from the property rental. Perhaps you could have a menu with incentive prices – a reduction on the cost of lunches served and completed by 1 pm, say. In a busy area you could double the flow of customers and increase revenues substantially. And most of that increase is profit, since the overhead hasn't increased.

Making Things Happen

Look for a trigger to prompt action

You can base a sales call or campaign on absolutely anything. Devise some apparent relevance, and away you go. There follows a variety of lists, conveniently organised by category. Your task: go through the lists and relate them to your line of business.

To make it easier for you, I've put some boxes so you can indicate the impact of any of these triggers on what you do. You can choose a positive impact, a negative impact or 'who knows?'.

Then go back and look at the categories that deliver a positive impact and see what these triggers suggest. Use them as a prompt to help you devise a reason to make your proposition. You may be amazed.

You can use the negative-impact triggers as reminders of possible problem areas.

These triggers are just a set of ideas. There's no reason why you shouldn't apply the thinking to the more specialised areas of what you do. You can follow a similar format and develop your own triggers. If you are in the travel business, identify triggers that affect that. If you sell life insurance, what triggers affect you? You'll find some blanks at the end of this section to help you do this.

Way 62 Triggers – Your customer's business: results, structure

	Impact on you		
	Positive	Negative	?
• Annual meeting	☐	☐	☐
• Annual results, earnings	☐	☐	☐
• Quarterly results, earnings	☐	☐	☐
• Change in orders, volume	☐	☐	☐
• Change in turnover, sales, profits	☐	☐	☐
• Spin-offs	☐	☐	☐
• Liquidation	☐	☐	☐
• Relocation	☐	☐	☐
• Mergers and acquisitions	☐	☐	☐
• Refinancing	☐	☐	☐
• New financing, share, rights issue	☐	☐	☐
• New debt issue	☐	☐	☐
• Bank problems	☐	☐	☐
• Takeover target – hostile	☐	☐	☐
• Takeover target – friendly	☐	☐	☐
• Takeover activator – hostile	☐	☐	☐
• Takeover activator – friendly	☐	☐	☐
• Investment analysts' reports – negative	☐	☐	☐
• Investment analysts' reports – positive	☐	☐	☐
• Sudden price moves in stock market	☐	☐	☐

Way 63 Triggers – your customer's business: management issues

	Impact on you		
	Positive	Negative	?
• Change in management	☐	☐	☐
• Newly elected committees	☐	☐	☐
• Crisis	☐	☐	☐
– Quality, product safety	☐	☐	☐
– Extortion	☐	☐	☐
– Accident, disaster	☐	☐	☐
– Management problems	☐	☐	☐
• Mission statement	☐	☐	☐
• Culture change	☐	☐	☐
• Employee morale	☐	☐	☐
• Quality control problems, product recalls	☐	☐	☐
• Low productivity	☐	☐	☐
• Factory, office, branch shut-down	☐	☐	☐
• Factory, office, branch relocation	☐	☐	☐
• Corporate image problems	☐	☐	☐
• New corporate identity	☐	☐	☐
• New advertising	☐	☐	☐
• New Internet Web-site	☐	☐	☐
• Sponsorship	☐	☐	☐
• Legal, regulatory problems	☐	☐	☐

Way 64 Triggers – Your customer's business: employment issues

	Impact on you		
	Positive	Negative	?
● Increase in workforce	☐	☐	☐
● New senior people hired	☐	☐	☐
● New university intakes	☐	☐	☐
● New appointments advertised	☐	☐	☐
● New appointments announced	☐	☐	☐
● Company intern programmes	☐	☐	☐
● Management conferences, courses	☐	☐	☐
● Training/Retraining programmes	☐	☐	☐
● Investors in people	☐	☐	☐
● Skills shortage	☐	☐	☐
● Industrial disputes, strikes	☐	☐	☐
● New union contracts	☐	☐	☐
● Redundancies, lay-offs	☐	☐	☐
● Staff turnover/attrition rate	☐	☐	☐
● Wage freeze	☐	☐	☐
● Salary reduction programme	☐	☐	☐
● Golden parachutes	☐	☐	☐
● Voluntary retirements	☐	☐	☐
● Pension plans	☐	☐	☐

Way 65   Triggers – Your customer's business: products and services

	Impact on you		
	Positive	Negative	?
• Company roadshows	☐	☐	☐
• New product launches	☐	☐	☐
• Brand repositioning	☐	☐	☐
• Brand advertising programmes	☐	☐	☐
– Television	☐	☐	☐
– Print	☐	☐	☐
– Radio	☐	☐	☐
– Outdoor/Transport	☐	☐	☐
– Theatrical	☐	☐	☐
– Direct mail	☐	☐	☐
• Sales promotion activities	☐	☐	☐
• Direct marketing	☐	☐	☐
• New Internet Web-site	☐	☐	☐
• Deadline projects	☐	☐	☐
• New contracts	☐	☐	☐
• Contracts lost	☐	☐	☐
• ISO 9000 quality programme	☐	☐	☐
• New branch opening	☐	☐	☐
• New retail outlet	☐	☐	☐
• Mature, tired product	☐	☐	☐
• New distributors	☐	☐	☐
• New selling techniques	☐	☐	☐

Way 66   Triggers – Economy

	Impact on you		
	Positive	Negative	?
• Interest rates up	☐	☐	☐
• Interest rates down	☐	☐	☐
• Unemployment up	☐	☐	☐
• Unemployment down	☐	☐	☐
• Inflation rate up	☐	☐	☐
• Inflation rate down	☐	☐	☐
• Mortgage rate up	☐	☐	☐
• Mortgage rate down	☐	☐	☐
• Balance of payments up	☐	☐	☐
• Balance of payments down	☐	☐	☐
• Income tax up	☐	☐	☐
• Income tax down	☐	☐	☐
• Tax relief improved	☐	☐	☐
• Tax relief reduced	☐	☐	☐
• Sales tax/VAT up	☐	☐	☐
• Sales tax/VAT down	☐	☐	☐
• Excise tax up	☐	☐	☐
• Excise tax down	☐	☐	☐
• Local tax/rates up	☐	☐	☐
• Local tax/rates down	☐	☐	☐
• Exchange rates up	☐	☐	☐
• Exchange rates down	☐	☐	☐
• Currency devaluation	☐	☐	☐

- Currency revaluation ☐ ☐ ☐
- Bankruptcies up ☐ ☐ ☐
- House prices up ☐ ☐ ☐
- House prices down ☐ ☐ ☐

Way 67   Triggers – Politics

	Impact on you		
	Positive	**Negative**	**?**
General election	☐	☐	☐
Local election	☐	☐	☐
By-election	☐	☐	☐
Change in national government	☐	☐	☐
Change in local government	☐	☐	☐
Political conference	☐	☐	☐
House of Commons	☐	☐	☐
House of Lords	☐	☐	☐
Honours lists	☐	☐	☐
New Prime Minister	☐	☐	☐
Members of Parliament	☐	☐	☐
European Community	☐	☐	☐
Congress (USA)	☐	☐	☐
Senate (USA)	☐	☐	☐
New President/Vice President (USA)	☐	☐	☐

Way 68   Triggers – Personal/Family

	Impact on you		
	Positive	**Negative**	**?**
• Birth	☐	☐	☐
• Marriage	☐	☐	☐
• Divorce	☐	☐	☐
• Retirement	☐	☐	☐
• Death	☐	☐	☐
• Suicide	☐	☐	☐
• Illness	☐	☐	☐
• Children	☐	☐	☐
• Mother	☐	☐	☐
• Father	☐	☐	☐
• Single parent	☐	☐	☐
• Parents	☐	☐	☐
• Grandparents	☐	☐	☐
• Siblings	☐	☐	☐
• Sister	☐	☐	☐
• Brother	☐	☐	☐
• Adoption/foster child	☐	☐	☐
• Uncle	☐	☐	☐
• Aunt	☐	☐	☐
• Cousins	☐	☐	☐
• In laws	☐	☐	☐
• Step-(brother, etc)	☐	☐	☐
• Half-(brother, etc)	☐	☐	☐
• Old people	☐	☐	☐

- Schools/University/Exams ☐ ☐ ☐
- Half term ☐ ☐ ☐
- School holidays ☐ ☐ ☐

Way 69   Triggers – Lifestyle

	Impact on you		
	Positive	Negative	?
New house	☐	☐	☐
New car	☐	☐	☐
Holidays	☐	☐	☐
Travel	☐	☐	☐
Timesharing	☐	☐	☐
Commuting	☐	☐	☐
Crime	☐	☐	☐
Bankruptcy	☐	☐	☐
Illness/Health Service/Hospitals	☐	☐	☐
Nursing homes	☐	☐	☐
Retirement	☐	☐	☐
Insurance	☐	☐	☐
Recycling	☐	☐	☐
Shopping	☐	☐	☐
– High street	☐	☐	☐
– Malls/Centres	☐	☐	☐
– Department stores	☐	☐	☐
– By mail	☐	☐	☐
DIY	☐	☐	☐
Supermarkets	☐	☐	☐

	Positive	Negative	?
• Food	☐	☐	☐
• Restaurants	☐	☐	☐
• Car boot sales	☐	☐	☐

Way 70 Triggers – Entertainment/ Communication

	Impact on you		
	Positive	Negative	?
• Television	☐	☐	☐
• Video, cassette	☐	☐	☐
• Satellite/Cable TV	☐	☐	☐
• Radio	☐	☐	☐
• Music	☐	☐	☐
• Stereo	☐	☐	☐
• Compact disk (CD)	☐	☐	☐
• Tape, cassette	☐	☐	☐
• Records	☐	☐	☐
• Home entertainment centre	☐	☐	☐
• Cinema	☐	☐	☐
• Theatre	☐	☐	☐
• Library	☐	☐	☐
• Books	☐	☐	☐
• Magazines	☐	☐	☐
• Newspapers	☐	☐	☐
• Computers/CD-Rom	☐	☐	☐
• Internet	☐	☐	☐
• Telephones/fax/mobile phones	☐	☐	☐

- Video games ☐ ☐ ☐
- Museums ☐ ☐ ☐
- Art galleries ☐ ☐ ☐
- Exhibitions ☐ ☐ ☐
- Theme parks ☐ ☐ ☐
- Sports ☐ ☐ ☐
  - Spectator ☐ ☐ ☐
  - Participatory ☐ ☐ ☐

Way 71   Triggers – Seasonal/Holidays

	Impact on you		
	Positive	Negative	?
Christmas Day (25 December)	☐	☐	☐
Boxing Day (26 December)	☐	☐	☐
New Year's Eve (31 December)	☐	☐	☐
New Year's Day (1 January)	☐	☐	☐
St Valentine's Day (14 February)	☐	☐	☐
April Fool's Day (1 April)	☐	☐	☐
St George's Day (23 April)	☐	☐	☐
Good Friday (varies)	☐	☐	☐
Easter (varies)	☐	☐	☐
Passover (varies)	☐	☐	☐
Independence Day, USA (4 July)	☐	☐	☐
Mother's Day	☐	☐	☐
Father's Day	☐	☐	☐

- Guy Fawkes Night   ☐   ☐   ☐
  (5 November)
- Hannukah (varies)   ☐   ☐   ☐
- Leap Year (1988, 1992, 1996,   ☐   ☐   ☐
  2000, 2004)
- Bank holidays   ☐   ☐   ☐
- Saints' days   ☐   ☐   ☐
- Ramadan   ☐   ☐   ☐
- Diwali   ☐   ☐   ☐

Way 72   Triggers – Weather

	Impact on you		
	Positive	Negative	?
Spring	☐	☐	☐
Summer	☐	☐	☐
Winter	☐	☐	☐
Autumn	☐	☐	☐
Summer time change (clocks forward)	☐	☐	☐
Greenwich time change (clocks back)	☐	☐	☐
Too hot	☐	☐	☐
Too cold	☐	☐	☐
Too wet	☐	☐	☐
Too dry	☐	☐	☐
Too windy	☐	☐	☐
Too stormy	☐	☐	☐
Too much pollution, smog	☐	☐	☐

- Pollen count too high   ☐   ☐   ☐
- Too much radiation (news reports)   ☐   ☐   ☐
- Global warming/greenhouse effect   ☐   ☐   ☐

Way 73   Triggers – Do your own thing

	Impact on you		
	Positive	Negative	?
_____	☐	☐	☐
_____	☐	☐	☐
_____	☐	☐	☐
_____	☐	☐	☐
_____	☐	☐	☐
_____	☐	☐	☐
_____	☐	☐	☐
_____	☐	☐	☐
_____	☐	☐	☐
_____	☐	☐	☐
_____	☐	☐	☐
_____	☐	☐	☐
_____	☐	☐	☐
_____	☐	☐	☐
_____	☐	☐	☐
_____	☐	☐	☐
_____	☐	☐	☐
_____	☐	☐	☐

Look at How You Come Across

Procter & Gamble's Head and Shoulders anti-dandruff shampoo had a brilliant slogo: 'You only get one chance to make a first impression.' There's lots of truth in that statement, no matter what you do. So an important part of getting more business means looking the part of someone who *gets* more business. And acting as if you are a success. Speaking with a quaver in your voice, you know, and saying 'you know' at the end of every other sentence, you know, does not bespeak the ideal image.

You need to look the part, speak the part and act the part. The least you can do is spend a bit of time in the dressing room before you go on stage, making sure you look the part. And you need to go over your lines. Presumably you've rehearsed these many times, so they should come almost automatically, but if you haven't, understand that rehearsal and role playing are essential. It is far better that you find out your embarrassing shortcomings and lack of answers in a non-threatening environment.

Way 74   Look the part

Dress according to the image of a successful person in your business. This may mean a three-piece suit, a set of overalls, a uniform or casual attire. But whatever it is, it needs to be clean and have that cared-for look.

If you deal with business people in offices, a classic suit is most appropriate. If you're behind the counter in a service business, perhaps a smart blazer or uniform jacket will work best. Think of the most successful businesses like your own, and think about how their best people look. Look no worse. In fact, look better.

Shiny shoes, neat hair, clean hands and fingernails; if you're a clean-shaven man, at least have the decency to have shaved! And smile! First impressions *do* count! Your appearance might well be the first human manifestation of your business. Don't make it the last.

Way 75   Speak the part

Be knowledgeable about your subject. There's nothing that destroys your credibility faster than a blank stare and a quizzical look in answer to a simple question.

Why do all unsuccessful salespeople have round shoulders and flat foreheads? Because when you ask them a question they shrug, and say, 'I don't know!' And when you work out the answer yourself and tell them, they slap their foreheads in amazement and say, 'Oh yes, that's it!'

Avoid jargon. Unless you are talking to a person who is even more technically competent than yourself, using jargon, especially with an uninformed customer, is showing off. Customers must not feel that you are putting them at a disadvantage. (Of course, there are whole industries based upon this sales technique.)

If you must use jargon, ask the customer if he or she understands what you mean when you do and explain the word or phrase if necessary. Of course, using slang while manifesting the dreaded 'you know' disease is the ultimate insult. If the mark, you know, had any, you know, clever bits he'd scram, you know?

If he had any *real* clever bits, in fact, he'd say, 'No, I don't know, and obviously neither do you! Cheerio!' Help to stamp out this dreadful trait once and for all!

Way 76   Act the part

The only surprises you may allow your customers to experience are pleasant ones. Realise that every untoward experience is a step closer to 'no deal'. You want constantly to bring yourself into the realm of 'yes deal'. This means that customers' expectations should be constantly raised by good experiences, and each new experience should raise their expectations further.

It's as though you're always raising the bar. As they jump each hurdle towards satisfaction, they contemplate the next one as being at roughly the same level as the last one, but you discreetly raise it and, through your own interaction, let them experience the joy of jumping higher than they thought they could. Then they start thinking, 'This is different. This is better. I like this.'

Think back to the best two or three sales experiences you ever had as a *customer*. Reflect on how you felt afterwards. Was there not a feeling of satisfaction and reward beyond that of getting the product or service you wanted? Good salespeople love to be sold. Relish every good buying experience and see what you can learn from it. It makes sense to write down a few thoughts to remind you of the key points in the future.

You'll surely find that your good feelings relate to having dealt with a person who understood your needs, understood the possible solutions and presented them in the most informative and convincing way.

What it boils down to is professionalism and a genuine interest in serving customers' needs. Ask yourself, 'Am I here because they are there, or are they there because I am here?' The answer will reveal all.

Way 77   Be enthusiastic

Nobody likes a moaner. Enthusiasm is contagious, and can certainly help to make the sale. A few months ago, I was in the bookshop at London's Gatwick Airport, on my way into town. I usually take the opportunity to check on the display of my books on the Kogan Page spinner rack. Imagine my surprise and delight to find a woman browsing through my latest epic, *101 Ways to Generate Great Ideas*! I paused for a moment, and then went up to her and said, with a big smile, 'Now that's a *really good* book!' She looked up at me and said, 'It is?' 'Yes,' I replied. 'I wrote it, see?' and I showed her my business card. 'Oh, that's amazing!' she said. I replied, 'I'll tell you what, you buy it and I'll *sign* it for you!' 'Okay,' she said. 'It'll make a good Christmas present for my husband.'

In New York I used to work with a man known as 'The Silver Fox', real name David Palmer, who then ran the Merrill

Lynch office in Boston. A conversation would usually start something like this: 'Hi, Dave, how ya doin'?' He would reply: '*Terrific!* – Slightly below par!' I must admit I've used the line a few times myself.

There is such a thing as too much enthusiasm and helpfulness. A French Count, an English Duke and a Polish engineer were about to go to the guillotine during the French Revolution. The Frenchman stepped forward. 'Have you any last words?' he was asked. 'The aristocrats shall live on!' he replied. He was quickly bundled on to the deadly machine, and the lever was pulled. The blade dropped and, miraculously, stopped just short of his neck. 'It is an Act of God. Set him free!' shouted the *chef de l'execution*. The Englishman was then similarly questioned. 'Royalty for ever!' he replied. He was placed on the chopping block and, miracle of miracles, as before, the blade stopped short. 'It is an Act of God. Set him free!' shouted the *chef de l'execution* again. Finally, the Polish engineer was ushered forth. 'Do you have any last words?' 'No, but I can show you what's wrong with your machine!' Yes, you can have *too much* enthusiasm.

Way 78   Be optimistic

Pessimism drags everyone down. When you are in a selling mode, pessimism can do nothing for you. Of course, you might be pessimistic and dealing with a customer who is *really* pessimistic, in which case you will come across as relatively optimistic!

The issue is, you need to be conditioned to success, not failure. If you know you're not going to make the sale, your prediction will come true. If you know you're going to make it, it *might* come true.

There are lots of 'laws' that address this. Here are some. Know the enemy!

- *Murphy's Law (aka Sod's Law)*
  If anything can go wrong, it will, and at the worst possible time.

- *The Opposing Laws of Expectations*
  Negative expectations yield negative results.
  Positive expectations yield negative results.

- *Foster's Train Traveller's Law*
  If you're early for the train it will be late arriving.
  If you're 30 seconds late for the train, it left on time.
- *The First Law of Motorway Madness*
  The other lane moves faster. This is inviolable.
- *The Second Law of Motorway Madness*
  If you change lanes to compensate, the one you left will immediately move faster (see *First Law*).
- *Hovis's Law of Buttered Toast*
  The likelihood of a piece of toast falling butter-side down is proportional to the value of the carpet.
- *Marconi's Three Laws of Broadcasting*
  1. If you turn the radio on and they're playing a song you really like, it is within five seconds of the end.
  2. If it is a song you really hate, it has just started.
  3. If it is a song you have never heard before and you love it at first hearing, they will not tell you what it is called at the end, and if you phone them to find out, they have lost the log sheets.

Way 79 Use positive language

It's interesting how often we hear people using negative language to describe things. It goes back to 'Are you part of the problem or part of the solution?' See how these examples illustrate that, with positive versions beneath them:

- – 'We don't have it in stock.' (= part of problem)
- + 'I can have one for you this afternoon. Would you like it delivered?' (= part of solution)

- – 'The film has already started playing. You'll miss the opening.' (= part of problem)
- + 'The next screening is at 9 o'clock.' (= part of solution)

- – 'We close in five minutes.' (= part of problem)
- + 'May I help you to make your selection?' (= part of solution)

- 'We don't take credit cards.' (= part of problem)
+ 'If you prefer not to pay in cash, we could take a cheque.' (= part of solution)

The problem is it's natural for us to express difficulties in a negative way. So, as an exercise, pick five situations in your own business environment that are usually dealt with negatively, and translate them into positive responses (use part of problem/part of solution approach if it helps).

Way 80   Is what you are doing helping or hindering your success?

There are people who make things happen. There are people things happen to. And there are people who wonder what happened. In which category are you or do you want to be?

Everything you do moves you in a certain direction. Even standing still moves you in a direction – maybe of failure. You need to make sure that, to the greatest possible extent, what you do moves you in the direction of success.

- Making an extra prospecting call moves you in the direction of success
- Going home early, leaving the job to be picked up next time you get to it, does not

Let's look at some other unfortunately all-too-familiar hindrances to success:

- Keeping a customer waiting
- Keeping a customer waiting without any indication of how long before he or she'll be dealt with (worse)
- Not answering the phone right away
- Not showing up at the appointed hour
- Not giving an appointed hour ('He'll try to get there as soon as he can – it should be some time this week.')

- Not delivering as promised ('The job is not done until you have come up with a *really good* excuse as to why the job is not done.')
- Delivering the wrong goods
- Delivering faulty goods
- Fixing faulty goods and they still don't work
- Providing hazardous goods (eg life threatening)
- Delivering incomplete work
- Being unable to deliver on time, knowing this, but not advising the customer of the expected delay
- Not checking the finished article before delivery and handing over something that fails immediately on departure, after the shop is closed

Write down some of your favourite customer repellents:

_____

_____

_____

Now let's look at some helpful movements:

- Dropping in to see a competitor's activity
- Trying your competitors' products or services
- Reading your competitors' advertising and brochures
- Reading a trade magazine on your business
- Going to a trade show about your business
- Talking to your colleagues about what customers are saying
- Talking to your customers
- Asking your customers for feedback on your products or services
- Delivering ahead of time
- Exceeding expectations
- Saying thank you for business

List some of your favourite customer attractors:

_____

_____

_____

_____

_____

Way 81   Improve telephone techniques

Why is it that some people don't answer the phone right away when it's ringing? They look at it and glower. There seems to be an attitude that a phone call is not important. I was in Seeboard, the electrical retail store of south eastern England. There were perhaps three assistants in the shop who were all dealing with customers. The phone was ringing. And ringing – 40–50 rings. Nobody would answer it.

All it takes is a polite 'excuse me, let me answer this'. If necessary, the caller can be called back. But just to let it ring is exactly how not to get more business. Letting the phone ring is being part of the problem. Answering it is being part of the solution. Personally, when I'm phoning a retail establishment to get some information, or place an order, I let it ring six times, then I hang up. I may phone back later, but only if I wasn't able to get what I want elsewhere. I mean, what is the phone *for*?

Providing an answerphone or a 24-hour number is an obvious step in the right direction of good customer service. But another very important aspect is returning the phone call. I'm amazed at how often people don't return phone calls. I can understand bill collectors suffering from this problem. But somebody offering services? The winners are, and always will be, those who handle their telephones professionally and thoughtfully.

If you work for a large organisation and you are involved in selling your products and services, it might be interesting to play the customer and call in to see how you're treated. Are you given the runaround? Do people genuinely want to help you or just get rid of you?

Putting someone on hold should not mean seemingly everlasting banishment. Even if you have (ugh!) 'music on hold', the holdee should be advised *at least every 30 seconds* of their status (see Way 19).

Way 82   Recognise the importance of training

Airline pilots keep on training. Doctors keep on training. So what about you? You're reading this book, and you're this far into it, so I guess you recognise the need for it. And I'll say it anyway. Don't fall behind. Go to seminars, trade shows, exhibitions. Read the trade press. Read books like this. Listen to motivational tapes. Network, network, network. Constantly upgrade your skills and knowledge. There's nothing like a good training session to shake the cobwebs out.

Two firms I work with, Young & Rubicam Advertising and Burson-Marsteller Public Relations, both the leaders in their fields, believe in training to the very highest level. I was recently involved in a session where the students were the managing directors of all their regional companies. They're so successful, could it be they know something? Yes. They know they don't know *enough*! You never know enough. Training is one of their top priorities. It should be one of yours.

Prompting Bigger Sales as You Sell

There are many things you can do to prompt bigger sales at the customer interface – the moment when the customer is making the buying decision. What you need to do is identify ways to prompt an upgraded decision as the customer takes the plunge and says yes. He or she is already in buying mode. So what can be added to the shopping basket that would serve you both well?

You must do this carefully. If you are careless or insensitive, you can blow the whole thing.

Here are some examples.

Way 83   The old egg in the malted trick

Many years ago, an organisation dedicated to the marketing of eggs managed to obtain a substantial increase in sales by the expedient of getting the sales person to ask a simple question on taking an order.

The scene – a milk bar or soda fountain (this was in America). Customer comes in and orders a malted-milk shake.

Soda jerk (sales person): 'Would you like one egg or two in your malted, sir?'
Customer: 'Oh, just one, please.'

Result, another egg is sold. Putting an egg in a malted is normally an extra-price option.

See how much more dynamic the above line is than:

Soda jerk: 'Would you like an egg in it, sir?'
Customer: 'Oh, no thanks.'

It's the same concept as the life insurance salesperson uses to set up an interview: 'I can see you next Tuesday, or would Thursday be better for you?' 'How about 10 am, or would you prefer after lunch?'

Way 84 The sales assistant as adviser

My wife recently opened a new bank account, and was offered a choice of premiums as a reward. One of them was a videotape of an Indiana Jones film. As she pondered what to accept, the bank person said: 'The Indiana Jones tape seems to be the most popular.' Bingo! Another tough decision made. And another sale for Spielberg.

The raised eyebrow, the slight intake of breath, the hesitation – these can spell death to a product that the customer has picked out. This then leads the sales person to the target item, which is proferred in a side-by-side comparison.

A few years ago, I was in a shop looking for a colour TV. There was a wall of TVs, all tuned to the same channel. I was interested in a Sony, and I noticed that all the Sonys were turned off. I asked the assistant why this was so. 'Sony's picture is so superior, we wouldn't sell any of the other sets if we had it on!' No kidding, that's what he said! Yes, I bought a Sony. Was this some type of inverse product demonstration?

Way 85 The New York deli question

In a retail environment, is the sales assistant someone who takes the money and rings a cash register, or is there a suggestion of enhanced business to be encouraged? A line as simple as 'Do you need anything else?' said to every customer could increase sales substantially, versus the usual 'Thanks!' 'Cheers!' or 'Much obliged'.

We often have our minds in neutral when shopping for simple things. We get home and realise we forgot something. A prompt from the person behind the counter can change that. I call it the New York deli question. Buy a sandwich at a Big Apple delicatessen, and here's what happens: 'Liverwurst and swiss on rye, please.' 'What else?' 'A Diet Coke.' 'What else?' 'Bag of corn chips.' 'What else?' 'A banana.' 'What else?'

'Coffee, regular.' 'What else?' 'That's it, already!' 'Okay, okay!'

When I was at Merrill Lynch, my boss John Fitzgerald used the same technique. I would be reporting to him on some business matter, and I'd be finished. 'What else?' We'd cover a bit more ground. 'What else?' And more. 'What else?' I think he worked in a deli once!

Way 86 Offer a little more

We now switch to the exclusive bar off the lobby of one of the great international hotels.

Customer: 'Scotch and soda, please.'
Bartender: 'Single or double, sir?'
Customer: 'Make it a double.'

Note the bartender said 'single or *double*', not 'double or *single*'. The customer, who, at this moment, has the attention span of a gnat, remembers the last word and acts accordingly. And it goes on:

Bartender: 'Would you like some canapés with that, sir?'
Customer: 'Why not?'

In my very early career days, in Toronto, I was at a shop taking delivery of my first ever made-to-measure suit, which I think cost $59 (this was in the late 1950s). I was with a friend who had introduced me to the shop, and I was very excited. 'How about a nice shirt to go with that?' The shopkeeper put one into my hands. 'Eight bucks!' Yes, yes! 'And a pair of socks? Three bucks!' Yes! I was really in buying mode now. 'How about a nice new tie for a buck?' Yes, oh yes! I handed over $71.

After we left the shop, my friend could hardly contain himself. He was screaming with laughter: 'When he offered you that tie for a dollar, do you know what he did? He took it off a rack marked "Ties, Special, 50¢"!' Well, I'll be . . . But I still felt good, even if I had been ripped off a little. By the way, the shopkeeper had turned a $59 transaction into one for $71 – a 20 per cent increase. That's what I mean by offering a little more. The customer can always say no.

Way 87   Sell up, not down

I went into one of the stationery shops near me to get some paper for my laser printer. I asked for my usual brand. The assistant pointed to another package and said: 'This is a lot cheaper.' 'Is it the same weight?' I asked. 'Oh yes.' 'Okay, I'll take a couple of packages.' She had singlehandedly reduced the shop's sales by 40 per cent in this transaction. I got the paper home, and it was not satisfactory. It kept misfeeding and jamming the works of the printer. Why was she trying to save me money? I reckon it all goes back to 'the customer's interests come first'. But is it the customer's interest to save money and get a lousy result out of the printer?

Better to take the position that the customer should go for the best you have. If a customer asks for a generic brand, show the better-quality product and explain, through the use of benefits, why it makes a better buy. Present it as a question: 'Are you aware of this? Did you know it does that? That means it will do *this* for you. Would you prefer it?'

Or present, a choice. 'If you are interested in the lowest-cost tyres, we have these retreads. But if you want to stay alive, you might prefer this brand!'

Way 88   Find a way to show the wares that work

A problem faced by Merrill Lynch, with its dozens of financial services, was that their sales people, called financial counsellors (FCs), would get comfortable with just three or four product lines. No matter what your need was, the FC would have a solution from this fairly limited array. Meanwhile, the firm would come out with exciting new products, supported by attractive brochures, roadshows, videotapes, hotlines, you name it. How could they get through?

I was asked to address this issue by Ira Lewis, who was in charge of Corporate Services Marketing at the time. We came up with a nice solution. First came a 28-page brochure which I wrote called 'How Merrill Lynch Can Help You Run Your Business More Effectively'. It was organised into four broad areas:

- How to manage your assets more advantageously
- How to minimise your tax liability
- How to manage your employee-benefit plans more effectively
- How to finance your working assets and production equipment

Within each of these areas, there was a brief description of techniques and financial vehicles that could address these needs.

The book was well laid out, with plenty of photographs. But we knew the only people who would read it right through would be the proofreaders and the lawyers. Others would perhaps leaf through it, and take note of an item that seemed interesting. Or they wouldn't. FCs would simply add it to their reading pile.

We needed a way to make the book *work* – as a prompting device for a conversation between the FC and the client about a relevant business need and a relevant Merrill Lynch solution.

We came up with two additional components to make this happen, and happen it did!

The first was an eight-page booklet for the FC, called 'Business Profile Recorder'. This was to be completed by the FC over a period of a few weeks. It had questions and checklists that tracked the brochure. So on page 4, under Tax Minimisation, it said:

- Are there any short- or long-term capital gains that would be subject to tax if realised?

  ☐ Yes ☐ No ☐ Key 8

- Are there any capital losses available for carry-forward?

  ☐ Yes ☐ No ☐ Key 9

These key numbers were the secret. The FC would, on getting a positive response to a question, tick the key number and refer to component two, a pocket-sized plastic card, containing these key numbers and referring the FC to the relevant page in the brochure. So against key 8, the crib card said 'Dividend rollover programme, see page 10'. On page 10 of the brochure, the FC would find a write-up on the features and benefits of this solution. The conversation thus went:

FC: 'Harry, you know that red booklet I sent you last week ... "How Merrill Lynch Can Help You Run Your Business More Effectively"? You have it there? Good. I've got mine right here. Let's turn to page 10. See that item down at the bottom – Dividend rollover programme? Let's go through this together ...' And, amazingly, the FC would at last be reading a relevant part of the brochure, showing the client a relevant solution and opening the way to more new business. It worked!

Way 89   Offer a premium that ties the customer to you

Everyone likes something for nothing. The marked success of the airlines' frequent-flyer programmes in the less regulated parts of the world bears this out. You enrol in the programme and get bonus miles for joining up. Take trips in certain ways to get bonus mileage. I'll give you an example. I had to make trips from the New York area to San Antonio, Texas once or twice a month for several months. I enrolled in the Continental Airlines plan and thereafter only flew Continental to Texas. I made sure I always rented cars from National Rent-A-Car (an extra 500 miles with every rental). I always stayed at Sheraton hotels (an extra 500 miles with every booking). I made sure I flew one time when there was a bonus of triple mileage for all trips in May. Pretty soon, I had enough miles to fly myself, my wife and daughter to Cancun, Mexico for a five-day holiday – over $1200 in air-fare value. Their programme captured my loyalty and custom.

Everyone I know in the States who travels a lot is in one or more frequent-flyer programmes, and they always make their flight decisions based on the impact on their accumulations. One friend flies so much, she always has enough miles to upgrade to first class from the economy fare. A few months ago she and her daughter flew to Europe on the mileage earnings. So those airlines have her loyalty.

In the UK these programmes are becoming very popular too, notably the Air Miles programmes.

Sometimes people get it wrong. I went to a video rental store on Fulham Road in London, and wanted to take out four tapes. They actually *increased* the cost of rentals, the more you took out! No, thank you! I didn't bother to ask what their rationale was. They probably had some very logical reason, but clearly not one orientated to the customer.

Way 90   Accept plastic money

People tend to spend more when they're using a credit card. Or they tend to make the buying decision that they wouldn't have made without the credit card. The mere ability to use a credit card can mean the difference between the customer making a purchase or going somewhere else that *will* take a credit card. My local hardware store changed ownership about two years ago. The new proprietor started taking credit cards immediately. 'When people want to buy a lawnmower or a chain saw, they expect to be able to pay by credit card. I know they go where they can do that, because that's what I do.' His sales are way ahead of the previous owner's, who wouldn't take credit cards because he was 'against them'.

Taking plastic money can also be the difference between getting paid quickly by the bank or credit supplier and getting paid slowly from the customer via several bills, statements, reminders and 'cheques in the post'.

There's no reason why a non-retail establishment shouldn't take credit cards. I remember ordering the replication of 50 sets of colour slides for a client from a New York slide production house – one I hadn't dealt with before. The bill was to be about $800. When I gave them the order, they said 'We'll need the payment in advance, or you can put it on your American Express card.' How simple!

Way 91 Offer a bonus

A good way of reducing the price without seeming to is to offer a temporary volume discount, like these well-known retailing concepts:

'Buy two, get one free.'
'Buy one, get the second one for half price.'
'Free plastic back scratcher with every box of soap flakes.'

In my early days at Procter & Gamble of Canada, I spent a year conducting a series of in-store tests for the premium-development department. P&G is famous for testing *everything*. The objective was to test the relative appeal of different on-pack premiums. This was done by comparing how the product sold with a price discount compared to its sale with the selected premium – perhaps a can opener, or a ball-point pen taped to the package.

It was a dream assignment. Go into a pre-arranged selection of a dozen or so supermarkets, identify yourself, find the merchandise (usually ten cases of detergent – perhaps 120 packets), find a place to put up the display, open the cases, affix the price-off stickers to half the stock, tape the premium to the other half, put the two displays up side by side, pay the value of the price discount to the store manager, then check back every day to measure sales at each store.

What did I learn? Mostly people went for the money-off deal. In the down-market areas, they bought the discounted product and stole the premium off the other box as well. Sometimes a premium would click, but not very often. But move that forward a few years and see what the breakfast-cereal industry knows only too well. My young son makes all his cereal choices based on what's in the box, or what he can get with a few coupons from the side of the packet.

Way 92   Extend your opening hours

My hardware store recently started opening for a short time on Sundays, because the new video rental store next door did so. I asked the owner if it was worthwhile. 'Definitely. And I've got a very selfish reason for saying that. The revenues we produce in the two hours we're open on Sunday give me enough to enable me to hire a part-timer to come in on Mondays – a fairly slow day – and enable me to take a day off! But most important, we're open when our customers want us to be open.'

If you run a shop and you close at, say, 6 pm, what do you do if you've just shut the door and a customer comes up? He knocks on the window. Do you say 'We're closed' and point to the sign, or do you invite the customer in (after checking to make sure he isn't there to rob you)? Do you let the customer in only if he is known to you? Which treatment does the customer want? Can you afford to turn him away?

Way 93   Offer a loss leader

In a retail environment, the first thing you want is store traffic – people walking in the door. One legitimate way to do this is to offer a loss leader – something at a real bargain price. The customer comes in for the electric kettle at £5.99 and walks out with a washing machine at £399, as well. This takes good salesmanship. The naughty version of this is called *bait and switch*, in which the advertised item runs out of stock very fast (if it ever existed), and the customer is offered an alternative at a much higher price. 'We just sold the last one, but we have this very nice model at only £9.99. Would you prefer white or yellow?'

Way 94   Offer a new line relevant to the rest of what you do

My local newsagent started offering video rental films on a rack. I needed a blank video-cassette. 'No, we don't get much call for them. In fact, you're the third person I've said that to this week!'

But seriously – and he was – what are the parallel items to what you offer that customers might want when they want what you are selling? An estate agent can arrange a mortgage, insurance, even a moving service. Many post offices now sell stationery. But why shouldn't a travel agent sell luggage? Or a luggage store vacation wear? Or a bookshop reading glasses? Or a wine shop cheese? Or a cheese shop wine? Or a PR agency press clippings? Or a bank computer software for money management? Or a kite shop sunglasses? Or what else? Here's an idea prompter:

What I Do Now

What I Could Do That's Linked

_____   _____

_____   _____

_____   _____

_____   _____

Way 95   Offer a telephone order service and be quick about it!

If people want what you have to offer, can they order it by phone? Can they pay for it by credit card? Can you deliver it fast? Then what are you waiting for? In the best of all possible worlds, you want to offer a toll-free 0800 telephone number, seven-day, 24-hour answering, preferably by a live body, and very fast response. Computer software outlets have learned this well. They run ads in the relevant computer magazine. The ads offer the software, usually at a discount from suggested retail price, and fast delivery. Thanks to companies like Federal Express and DHL, goods ordered before, say, 4 pm can be in your hands by 10 am *the next morning*. Some companies even offer overnight delivery *free* if the order size is above a certain amount.

Should you do this yourself, or use a response service? The trouble with these services is, in the UK, they are quite expensive, especially when compared to the same service in the US. I recently checked this out and the equivalent services in each country cost twice as much in the UK as in the US. Perhaps as volume expands in this area and there is competition, the price will come down.

The ideal service will offer a telephone line, a trained operator to answer the phone and take the order, handle the credit card information and forward the order to you, probably direct to your computer. But the up-front charges and monthly minimums are so high that you have to have a very large volume, or a high-priced/high-profit item to justify the cost per call. It would be worth looking at the difference in cost between using a service and handling it from your own resources. At the very least, you could handle the calls live during the hours you are open and by recording machine after hours. But this is a second class option.

Beyond the toll-free 0800 number, there are other telephone services on offer. One is the 'Freephone' concept. Here the customer dials 100 (for the operator) and asks for Freephone Bloggs (or whatever codeword you've agreed on). The operator looks the linkage up and puts you through, charging the call to the outfit the customer wants to reach. Another service is the 0345 number. The customer dials a number prefixed with the code 0345. This puts him through and charges the customer for the call, but at local calling rates. The difference is paid by the other end.

Worst of all, from the customer's point of view, is the premium call (usually 0891). This is the opposite of a toll-free call. In the UK, at present, you can pay 50p or more per minute (40p off-peak) for the call. I think a company that merely offers its brochure to a customer has a lot of nerve doing so in this way. Somehow they make it take three minutes to get the data! Offering some useful information, on the other hand, might justify this type of service. In fact there's a whole industry offering these types of premium number.

Way 96 Don't wait until after they've budgeted

A lot of companies have rigorous budgeting procedures. The budgeting process takes place about three months before the start of their fiscal year. If what you offer will involve a major expenditure, you want to make sure you're in their budget. If you're not, you may find yourself waiting until next year for approval.

Make a note of your target's budgeting situation, and then make sure you've made your proposal in time to be included in the budget.

Way 97 Give a deadline for buying

People are notoriously unwilling to make a buying decision, so it may be up to you to create a deadline. 'I can hold this price until next Wednesday.' 'This stock is going back on Friday, after which I won't be able to offer you the same kind of deal.' 'I only have one left, and I'm reducing the price £100 a day until it's sold!' 'It's first come, first served, so if you want to be sure of having it, I'd advise you to buy it now.' 'This is a prepublication price. After 1 June, it will cost £5 more.'

Way 98 Play hard to get

Years ago in Toronto, you used to see huge queues outside the fashionable discothèques. And this was in winter, when outside meant many degrees below zero! On a rare occasion, I actually visited one of these establishments. When we finally got inside, I was amazed, and somewhat annoyed, to find the place practically empty. It was all a ploy, to create the impression of popularity.

Some years later, as a stockbroker, I was working in the Toronto office of Merrill Lynch, an American firm. Some of my clients were US citizens living in Canada. Over the New York wire came an offering of new Pan American Airways bonds (this was about 1969). One of my American clients liked Pan Am, and I phoned him. He gave me an order for $20,000 worth of bonds.

The next day I was on the carpet and severely reprimanded for selling a security in Canada that was not registered (ie, legal) there. I was to phone my client and tell him he could not have the bonds. 'But I'm an American!' he exploded. 'Why can't I buy bonds in our own Pan Am?' 'Because they are not for sale in Canada. I made a mistake. I should not have offered them to you.' Order cancelled, commission lost and $100 penalty for me.

Well, you guessed it. Nothing would stand in my client's way. He was an American and he was going to exercise his divine right to invest in an American company, and to hell with any silly Canadian laws. Two days later, he phoned and told me he had opened an account in Detroit and had bought the bonds. So there! I bet he wished he hadn't, since Pan Am is now bankrupt. Ah, well.

Way 99   Offer a reward to people who bring you business

Many of your networking contacts could be in a position to bring in some business to you. It is perfectly legitimate to offer them a fee or commission for doing so. Let this be known, discreetly. Alternatively, you could work out an incentive programme where you offer trade benefits. You get a sale, you give a discount in return. They bring you business, you give them office space. And so on.

Of course, this can work just as well in reverse. You may find that some of the people you see regularly can use the services of one of your networkees. Work out an arrangement where you are compensated. Backscratchers, anyone?

Way 100   Ask others what they do to get more business

Everybody has their own ways of developing business. Don't be afraid to ask. You may get a good idea. I make it a point to do so regularly. Last time it was a London cabbie. 'What do you do to get more business?' I asked. 'I go where the travellers are,' he said. 'Railway stations, hotels, airports, that sort of thing.' It reminds me of the famous bank robber who was asked, 'Why do you rob banks?' 'That's where the money is,' he replied.

Another enquiry of an electronics manufacturer brought the suggestion of an 'end-of-line clearance' – a reduced price incentive. Another said, 'It costs me four times as much to get a new customer as it does to keep an existing one. I concentrate on repeat business.' And another said, 'I never ask for just one referral. I always try to get at least three. And the best time to get a referral is from someone who's just turned you down. They need to assuage their guilt.'

Way 101 Cash the cheque

My wife worked for Atlantic Computers as a sales manager at the time of their demise in 1990. This was an enormous business failure, and many people suffered, she included (= me included!). But not as much as the young salesman who received a bonus cheque for something like £80,000 the day he was going on holiday. He went for a celebratory lunch, intending to bank the cheque on the way. But the bank was too busy, and he continued with his rather liquid lunch plans. By the time 'lunch' was over, the bank was closed. So he locked the cheque in his desk drawer at Atlantic and flew off to sunny climes. Two weeks later he returned. Atlantic was by now dead. So was the cheque.

The moral? What good is more business if you don't get paid?

Index